Daily Affirmations for Self-Love

2222 Positive Affirmations to attract happiness

by Amelia Bellesource

"Relaxed Guru" Books

© Copyright 2021 Amelia Bellesource All rights reserved.

This document is geared towards providing exact and reliable information concerning the topic and issue covered. The publication is sold with the idea that the publisher is not required to render accounting, officially permitted, or otherwise qualified services. If advice is necessary, legal or professional, a practiced individual in the profession should be ordered.

In no way is it legal to reproduce, duplicate, or transmit any part of this document in either electronic means or printed format. Recording of this publication is strictly prohibited, and any storage of this document is not allowed unless with written permission from the publisher. All rights reserved.

The information provided herein is stated to be truthful and consistent, in that any liability, in terms of inattention or otherwise, by any usage or abuse of any policies, processes, or directions contained within is the sole and utter responsibility of the recipient reader. Under no circumstances will any legal obligation or blame be held against the publisher for any reparation, damages, or monetary loss due to the information herein, either directly or indirectly. Respective authors own all copyrights not held by the publisher.

The information herein is offered for informational purposes solely and is universal as so. The presentation of the information is without a contract or any guarantee assurance.

The trademarks that are used are without any consent, and the publication of the mark is without permission or backing by the trademark owner. All trademarks and brands within this book are for clarifying purposes only and are owned by the owners themselves, not affiliated with this document.

Disclaimer

The content of this book has been checked and compiled with great care. For the completeness, correctness and topicality of the contents however no guarantee or guarantee can be taken over. The content of this book represents the personal experience and opinion of the author and is for entertainment purposes only. The content should not be confused with medical help.

There will be no legal responsibility or liability for damages resulting from counterproductive exercise or errors by the reader. No guarantee can be given for success. The author therefore assumes no responsibility for the non-achievement of the goals described in the book.

Table of Contents

INTRODUCTION TO AFFIRMATIONS — 1

YEAR 1: VERY SHORT AFFIRMATIONS FOR BEGINNERS — 2

YEAR 2: SHORT POSITIVE AFFIRMATIONS FOR ADVANCED BEGINNERS — 18

YEAR 3: POSITIVE AFFIRMATIONS FOR ADVANCED USERS — 34

YEAR 4: LONG POSITIVE AFFIRMATIONS FOR EXPERTS — 60

YEAR 5: VERY LONG POSITIVE AFFIRMATIONS FOR PROS — 87

FINANCIAL AFFIRMATIONS FOR EVERY DAY — 145

CONCLUSION: IT'S IMPORTANT THAT YOU REMEMBER TO TAKE CARE OF YOURSELF — 170

Join our "Relaxed Guru" email list to receive a **free mindfulness book** and stay informed about future books:

→ https://bit.ly/3bwF4vR ←

Introduction to Affirmations

You can change your life by reading this book for just a few minutes every day of the week. You will be more positive about yourself, your abilities and get rid of negativity from your life. It does not matter if you are stressed out at work or having problems with relationships – this book will help you immensely.

The "Daily Affirmations for Self-Love" book contains a collection of 2222 positive affirmations that will change your day, your week and hopefully your whole life. It has been written for people with a busy lifestyle so you can enjoy it anywhere and at any time. Most affirmations are short and easy to remember so they will only take a few seconds out of your day. Some are longer, so you can read them on your way to work or while you are having breakfast. There are even some affirmations that are split into two parts, this is because they have more impact when you say them twice.

It has been written in a way that makes you think of new things every day so your mind will be active and improve with every affirmation. If there is one thing I hope to achieve from this book, it is for people to feel different about themselves. To feel empowered, motivated and inspired. If you have ever read any books on self- development, you will know that it is all too easy to forget about them the next day. With every affirmation I have tried to build in some sort of reminder or trigger so that they will stick with you for longer.

Because it is an issue for many people's happiness, we've included a separate section with financial affirmations in addition to the positive ones. If you don't like this, stick to chapters 1-5.

If you think that this book might be useful for someone in your life then please share it with them, thanks!

Year 1: Very short Affirmations for Beginners

1) I am calm.

2) I am unique.

3) Life is fun.

4) Life is good.

5) Life loves me.

6) I am priceless.

7) I am confident.

8) I love my life.

9) I will never give up.

10) I trust my gut.

11) My life is fun.

12) I love being me.

13) I love to laugh.

14) I love me for me.

15) I find my own way.

16) I am free to be ME.

17) I am safe and secure.

18) I am safe and loved.

19) I am worthy of love.

20) My life is abundant.

21) Today is a good day.

22) I am already perfect.

23) Life is my playground.

24) I can do hard things.

25) I live in beautiful and exciting world.

26) I deserve to be happy.

27) I deserve to be loved.

28) I am the embodiment of life.

29) My life is a work of art.

30) Love is all around me.

31) My life has a purpose.

32) Greatness is within me.

33) I am a wonderful person.

34) I live with ease today.

35) I love new experiences.

36) I make plenty of money.

37) My best is yet to come.

38) Today is a fresh start.

39) My growth is inevitable.

40) Self-love is self-care.

41) All is well in my world.

42) I trust the flow of life.

43) I am strong and capable.

44) I am surrounded by love.

45) The best is yet to come.

46) I am a daydream believer.

47) I am enough just as I am.

48) Things are going well in my world.

49) I'm starting fresh today.

50) It's a great day because.

51) I am loved by many people.

52) My thoughts are valuable.

53) Today is a new beginning.

54) My day is looking good.

55) I am able and trustworthy.

56) I am fearless and capable.

57) I am in love with my life.

58) My home is a safe haven for me to relax in.

59) I attract positive things.

60) I have a smooth day today.

61) I love and forgive myself.

62) Life is good to me always.

63) Life loves me and so do I.

64) Oh, what a wonderful world.

65) Today, I choose happiness.

66) Today, I will be positive.

67) Happiness is within me now.

68) I allow myself to be happy.

69) I always have a great idea.

70) I always have a smooth day.

71) I am letting go of the past

72) I am more than good enough.

73) I am talented beyond belief

74) I deserve the best in life.

75) I have unlimited potential.

76) Life loves me, and so do I.

77) My life will improve today.

78) People are inherently good.

79) Success is attracted to me.

80) Today is a day of miracles.

81) I am beautiful the way I am.

82) I have good ideas every day.

83) I trust the process of life.

84) If it scares you, go for it.

85) It's good to be alive today.

86) Life has incredible meaning.

87) My heart is filled with joy.

88) My past is a distant memory.

89) My thoughts create my world.

90) I build bridges, not walls.

91) Every day is a new beginning.

92) I am not alone in this world.

93) I radiate love wherever I go.

94) It feels good to be ME today.

95) My life is full of abundance.

96) My mind is quiet and focused.

97) The universe provides for me.

98) Who I am is who I need to be.

99) My life is full of miracles.

100) All is well in my world today.

101) I am good enough just as I am.

102) I can control my own thoughts.

103) I love myself unconditionally.

104) I will think positively today.

105) Life is an exciting adventure.

106) Life is full of possibilities.

107) Life loves me unconditionally.

108) Life is a love affair with no conditions.

109) My body is healthy and strong.

110) My day is looking great today.

111) My mind is quiet and at peace.

112) My natural state is happiness.

113) My thoughts create my reality.

114) The world is an amazing place.

115) Today I am taking time for me.

116) Today, I choose to enjoy life.

117) What a wonderful day today is.

118) I always have more than enough.

119) I am doing the best that I can.

120) I deserve love and forgiveness.

121) I give and receive love easily.

122) Life does everything with love.

123) There's always a way around it.

124) My mind is quiet and at peace.

125) Everyday gets easier and better.

126) Everything happens for a reason.

127) I am grateful to be alive today.

128) I am thankful to be alive today.

129) I release the need for approval.

130) Life has been good to me lately.

131) My past no longer holds me back.

132) My thoughts are loving and kind.

133) The present is always right now.

134) Time is ticking. don't waste it.

135) Today is going to be a great day

136) A new day brings a new beginning.

137) All good things are headed my way

138) Each day is better than the last.

139) Great fortune comes my way today.

140) I allow myself to be happy today.

141) I am safe, laid back and relaxed.

142) I am surrounded by loving people.

143) I have a deep respect for myself.

144) I have all the time in the world.

145) I love the life that I am living.

146) Life is an adventure and so am I.

147) Life is full of beauty and magic.

148) Life is moving forward every day.

149) My creativity flows effortlessly.

150) My life has a meaningful purpose.

151) My past does not equal my future.

152) Success flows easily to me today.

153) This has been a great day so far.

154) This will be a great day because.

155) Today is going to be a great day.

156) Today is the best day of my life.

157) Today, I am going to love myself.

158) All good things are headed my way.

159) Every day of my life is a miracle.

160) Good things happen to good people.

161) Good things happen to good people.

162) I am a strong and powerful person.

163) I am grateful for my healthy body.

164) I am secure, strong, and powerful.

165) I expect good things in my future.

166) I have the power to change myself.

167) Life has given me all that I need.

168) My body is healthy, fit, and trim.

169) Life is always working out for me.

170) Life makes sense to me, every day.

171) Life opens doors for me every day.

172) Life has always been a smooth ride for me.

173) I am a unique and remarkable person.

174) The past does not equal the future.

175) The universe is taking care of me.

176) Today is going to be a fantastic day.

177) I am a unique and beautiful person.

178) I am capable of achieving my goals.

179) I am confident in my own abilities.

180) I am filled with happiness and joy.

181) I am filled with health and energy.

182) I am grateful for the little things

183) I am in charge of my own happiness.

184) I feel good about myself right now.

185) I live the life of my dreams today.

186) My family loves me unconditionally.

187) My life is a story only I can write.

188) My life is full of positive energy.

189) My life is unfolding in perfection.

190) This is going to be an amazing day.

191) Today I choose to do something fun.

192) Today is a new day full of wonders.

193) Today, I let go of my past regrets.

194) I am confident, strong and powerful.

195) I am grateful for the little things.

196) I am loved and love unconditionally.

197) I am safe, healthy, and happy today.

198) I can relax easily and effortlessly.

199) I feel like a million dollars today.

200) I give thanks for the little things.

201) I love my life, today and every day.

202) I love to watch my children grow up.

203) My business is thriving and growing.

204) My dreams are coming true right now.

205) My life is full of joy and laughter.

206) My mind is open to all possibilities

207) My thoughts are creating my reality.

208) People like me and enjoy my company.

209) People on my team support me always.

210) The more I smile, the happier I get.

211) I am enjoying the process of my life.

212) Today, my mind is sharp and focused.

213) Every day, my life is getting better.

214) Everything is working out for me now.

215) I always have more than enough money.

216) The more I smile, the luckier I get.

217) I deserve the best life has to offer.

218) I love myself just the way that I am.

219) I never lose... I either win or learn.

220) Life is treating me kindly every day.

221) My happiness is very important to me.

222) My life is constantly getting better.

223) My life is full of happiness and joy.

224) My love fills countless hearts today.

225) The power to change my life is in me.

226) This moment is full of possibilities.

227) Today, all my dreams are coming true.

228) Today, I am healthy in body and mind.

229) Today, I take back control of myself.

230) I am a confident and smart individual.

231) I am open to receiving wonderful news.

232) I am surrounded by people who love me.

233) I give thanks for the love in my life.

234) Life is a game and I know how to play.

235) Life is an adventure - I am living it.

236) Life is giving me exactly what I need.

237) My life is full of joy and prosperity.

238) My success increases every single day.

239) The harder I work, the luckier I get.

240) All of my relationships are harmonious.

241) All the power of life is within me now.

242) And in the end… everything will be okay.

243) Each breath brings life and good health

244) Every day, I love myself more and more.

245) Good people are always attracted to me.

246) Good things only happen to good people.

247) I am a beautiful person inside and out.

248) I am strong enough to let life live me.

249) I look forward to each new opportunity.

250) I make decisions easily and grow daily.

251) It's easy to take care of myself today.

252) Life is opening doors for me every day.

253) Life is unfolding in divine perfection.

254) My life gets better as each day goes by.

255) My life is full of wonderful surprises.

256) My mind is quiet and filled with peace.

257) My partner loves me for who I truly am.

258) Others see me as beautiful and lovable.

259) Today is filled with happiness and joy.

260) Today will be filled with good fortune.

261) Today, my mind continues to grow wiser.

262) Every day brings more peace into my life

263) Everyone in my life is working out well.

264) Good health is a result of good choices.

265) I am at peace with where I am right now.

266) I am free to follow my own path in life.

267) I am grateful for this moment right now.

268) I am learning life-long lessons quickly.

269) I am successful in all areas of my life.

270) I am successful in everything that I do.

271) I am willing to see the good in my life.

272) I can do anything that I put my mind to.

273) I love and accept myself unconditionally.

274) I love myself exactly the way that I am.

275) If I believe in myself, who can stop me?

276) Life loves me and is treating me kindly.

277) Life loves me, so I can love myself too.

278) Love surrounds me with warmth every day.

279) My body feels healthier every single day

280) My family and friends support me always.

281) My relationships are healthy and loving.

282) Success and abundance are my birthright.

283) The biggest risk of all? Not taking one.

284) The more you smile. the happier you get.

285) Today, I have a new perspective on life.

286) Today's worries are tomorrow's memories.

287) You are not alone. I'm here to help you.

288) Success is the game I was born to play.

289) Every day I am getting better and better.

290) Health grows stronger as each day passes.

291) I am successful day by day, step by step.

292) I can do anything if I put my mind to it.

293) I choose happiness over worry every time.

294) I deserve all the abundance in the world.

295) I have no need for negativity in my life.

296) Life is moving smoothly for me right now.

297) My happiness brings me great friendships.

298) My joy multiplies exponentially every day.

299) My life is full of endless possibilities.

300) My life is full of success and happiness.

301) My optimism makes this day the best ever.

302) Today, all of my needs are met perfectly.

303) All the knowledge I need is within me now.

304) I am exactly where I need to be right now.

305) I am valuable and worthwhile just as I am.

306) It is safe for me to be my authentic self.

307) It is safe for me to express myself fully.

308) Life does everything with love, every day.

309) Money comes to me easily and effortlessly.

310) My body is a temple of my soul and spirit.

311) My life is full of beauty and grace today.

312) My life is unfolding exactly as it should.

313) My mind dances with wonderful ideas today.

314) My mind has the power to control my moods.

315) Positive energy brings out the best in me.

316) Successful people think positive thoughts.

317) The future brings only good things my way.

318) The better I do the better my life gets.

319) The world loves me just the way that I am.

320) Today, I release stress and embrace peace.

321) Today, I'll do something to improve myself

322) All of my dreams are coming true right now.

323) Being in a good mood is the only way to go.

324) I am a go-getter and do not give up easily.

325) I am a magnet for good health and wellness.

326) I am diligent in creating my own happiness.

327) I am here now and that is all that matters.

328) I am intelligent, creative and resourceful.

329) I am loved and love others unconditionally.

330) I am rich and successful, today and always.

331) I have a great family to support me always.

332) I trust myself to make it through anything.

333) I will never speak negatively about myself.

334) My life is full of unlimited possibilities.

335) Remember that you don't have to be perfect.

336) Success comes easily when you are positive.

337) The more good I do, the better my life becomes.

338) This is going to be a wonderful, happy day.

339) As I change my thoughts, I improve each day.

340) Every day is a new chance to make it better.

341) I deserve all good things life has to offer.

342) Life loves me unconditionally, just as I am.

343) Loving myself brings out the best in others.

344) My positive attitude brings me great things.

345) They may not like me but I'm still doing me.

346) This too shall pass. Everything always does.

347) Today, I feel so much better than yesterday.

348) Today only good things are going to happen.

349) Everyday life gives me opportunities to grow.

350) Everyone has their own path and I am on mine.

351) He may never know it but he made me stronger.

352) I can create anything that I want in my life.

353) I have clear goals and a purpose for my life.

354) Life is always giving me exactly what I need.

355) Life is moving forward smoothly for me today.

356) Life is so much better when you are positive.

357) My optimism will make this day the best ever.

358) The more good I do, the luckier my life gets.

359) The more positive things I say, the better my life gets.

360) The more positive I am, the luckier I become.

361) There are many ways that life loves me today.

362) There are many ways that life loves me today.

363) Things really go my way when I stay positive.

364) We all deserve happiness, peace love in life.

365) Every day that goes by, my optimism increases.

Year 2: Short Positive Affirmations for Advanced Beginners

366) I appreciate all that is in my life right now.

367) I attract success with my thoughts and energy.

368) I can achieve anything if I put my mind to it.

369) I let go of my past and focus on the positive.

370) It's okay to ask for help. believe me, I know.

371) Love flows through me and around me every day.

372) My life is always getting better in every way.

373) My mind is quieter than it's ever been before.

374) Remember that nobody is perfect. not even you.

375) The past is behind me...behind me...BEHIND me.

376) The world loves me and can't get enough of me.

377) This, too, shall pass. Everything always does.

378) Today is beautiful with all its possibilities.

379) Failure is the rocket fuel I need to succeed.

380) My deepest desires are now coming into being.

381) All of my relationships are healthy and loving.

382) Every day brings me closer to self-realization.

383) Everything that happens is for my highest good.

384) Good things are happening in my life right now.

385) I am surrounded by beautiful things and people.

386) I can learn anything I set my mind to learning.

387) I have a deep connection with the flow of life.

388) I have so many things to be grateful for today.

389) I love all the qualities that make up who I am.

390) My body is healthy, fit, slim, trim, wonderful.

391) Optimism is a state of mind. and so is success.

392) Riches come naturally into my experience today.

393) The only person who can work out my life is ME.

394) The only way to have a bad day is to think one.

395) Today will be a great day because I make it so.

396) What others think of me is none of my business.

397) If you stay positive, good things will follow.

398) All of the guidance I need comes from within me.

399) Each breath brings me closer to positive change.

400) Every breath that makes my lungs expand with air

401) I always get to where I am going, and much more.

402) I am at peace with the way things are right now.

403) I am attracting better relationships in my life.

404) I am the master of my own destiny & no one else.

405) I deserve happiness, love, and prosperity today.

406) I only have positive things to say about myself.

407) If we all work together, there's no stopping us.

408) I'm becoming more and more optimistic every day.

409) It's been a good day and I am grateful for that.

410) Love comes into my life easily and effortlessly.

411) My body heals itself naturally every single day.

412) New ideas are flowing easily into my mind today.

413) Positive energy is what drives me forward today.

414) The power of good vibes is what drives me today.

415) The Universe brings me opportunities to succeed.

416) Today will be a great day because I make it one.

417) Today, my life is filled with happiness and joy.

418) I am going to break through all barriers today.

419) Every morning is a new day full of opportunities.

420) Everything that happens to me today will be good.

421) I am loved and cared for by my family and friends

422) I can accomplish anything if I put my mind to it.

423) I deserve love and happiness, so I accept it now.

424) Life is full of opportunities for new beginnings.

425) My heart is filled with all the love in the world

426) My worth is not based on what others think of me.

427) Peace flows through me every moment of every day.

428) All good things are happening in my life right now.

429) The Universe always provides exactly what I need.

430) The world is full of wonderful, beautiful people.

431) They're just words - so why not just ignore them?

432) This moment is filled with peace and tranquility.

433) Today is a golden opportunity for new beginnings.

434) We all deserve happiness, peace and love in life.

435) Today is wonderful because anything is possible.

436) Each breath brings me strength, courage, and love.

437) Every day, I step closer to my dreams coming true.

438) Good health is always flowing into and through me.

439) Growth is a natural product of embracing the truth

440) I am ready to move forward into a positive future.

441) I am the person I've been waiting for all my life.

442) I expect great things to happen today and they do.

443) I make smart decisions and follow my gut feelings.

444) It's time to break out of this rut - successfully.

445) Life is taking care of me...I don't have to worry.

446) My relationships are happy, loving and harmonious.

447) My thoughts are creating an abundant future for me

448) Nothing can stop me from achieving my goals today.

449) I'm a selfless person, and that is how I've been able to improve my life.

450) Trust your gut instincts. it's there for a reason.

451) When you expect goodness, goodness comes your way.

452) Today I will be better than what I was yesterday.

453) The better I behave, the happier and more fulfilled my life becomes.

454) Each new day brings me closer to the life I desire.

455) Each new day is a gift that I enjoy to the fullest.

456) Every moment is eternal bliss when I stay positive.

457) I am letting my light shine brightly in this world.

458) I am surrounded by people who love and care for me.

459) I feel excited about new experiences coming my way.

460) I have nothing to prove, and no one to prove it to.

461) I love who I've become and where life is taking me.

462) If you don't like where you are in life, change it.

463) Others are drawn to my positivity. It's contagious.

464) People are drawn to my positivity. it's contagious.

465) The Universe provides for me in amazing ways today.

466) There is no one to "fix." I am enough just as I am.

467) Growth is a natural product of embracing the truth

468) At this very moment, my life has never felt so good.

469) Everything happens for a reason and in its own time.

470) Everything in my life always works out for the best.

471) I am capable and deserving of having an amazing day.

472) I am good enough to achieve all my dreams and goals.

473) I love my life and feel joy in everything that I do.

474) I'm already great. So why not allow myself to shine.

475) My children are happy, healthy, smart, and thriving.

476) My life has an endless supply of happiness and love.

477) Today is a gift, that's why it's called the PRESENT.

478) Today is a new beginning with endless possibilities.

479) Today is another opportunity for renewal and growth.

480) Today, I face all of life's challenges with courage.

481) Every day brings new opportunities for me to succeed.

482) Every day that goes by brings more peace into my life

483) Every day there is a miracle taking place in my body.

484) Everyday, my body tells me how good it feels to live.

485) Expecting good things to happen is easy. and they do.

486) I have plenty of love to share with people around me.

487) I make plenty of money; however, I am happy and free.

488) It's always "my day" somewhere every day of the year.

489) Let them keep talking. I love hearing myself succeed.

490) Life is tough but that's where the diamonds are made.

491) My body heals itself faster than the doctor expected.

492) My relationship with my partner is a dream come true.

493) Only good comes from being positive. I know that now.

494) Positivity is all I see today. It's just that simple.

495) Success, happiness, love and peace are my birthright.

496) The more love I give away, the bigger my heart grows.

497) There is always a reason to be positive and grateful.

498) There is always more to learn and experience in life.

499) This moment is pure joy. And it keeps getting better.

500) Today is a new beginning...where anything can happen.

501) Today, I let go of my past and focus on the positive.

502) Every day in every way I am getting better and better.

503) I'm feeling more and more beautiful every day.

504) Everyday I'm getting stronger and wiser.

505) Every day of my life is filled with happiness and joy.

506) Every decision I make helps me become a better person.

507) Having a positive mental attitude gets me far in life.

508) I am lovable and loveable - exactly as I am right now.

509) I am not the same as yesterday but a 'better' version.

510) I deserve to be happy and that happiness starts today.

511) I handle each difficult situation with grace and ease.

512) I love myself unconditionally & so does everyone else.

513) I radiate my own inner light that brightens the world.

514) I think, feel, speak, and act positively all day long.

515) I'm already happy. So why don't we make today our day?

516) I'm excited about what life has in store for me today.

517) It's easy for me to let go of things I cannot control.

518) Loving myself helps me to be confident in my own skin.

519) My life feels like joy and ease and success right now.

520) Nothing can stop me from reaching my goals and dreams.

521) The Universe provides for me in amazing ways every day.

522) Today, all things are working out for my highest good.

523) Today, I focus on all the wonderful things in my life.

524) I feel blessed to be surrounded by kind people who are willing to take a chance on me.

525) I am growing from a cute little baby into an even more beautiful human being.

526) Every day is a new beginning with endless possibilities.

527) I am capable of achieving anything that is in my heart.

528) I have a lot to smile about. and so do those around me.

529) I let go of the past and live fully in this moment now.

530) I will find ways to make this day better than the last.

531) My body throbs with energy from eating nutritious food.

532) My life feels like joy and ease and success, right now.

533) Never give up. because there's always another tomorrow.

534) No matter how far away I may feel, this too shall pass.

535) The more love I give away, the bigger my heart becomes.

536) There are many different ways that life loves me today.

537) This is going to be a fabulous day. I can already tell.

538) Today I will be kind and gentle with myself and others.

539) You are enough. no matter who says or thinks otherwise.

540) All my worries and fears fade away when I stay positive.

541) All that I do is always working out for my highest good.

542) Every day is a good day. I am living my best life today.

543) Every day of my life gets better than the one before it.

544) Every moment, I have a chance to do something wonderful.

545) Everything about this moment is right. because I say so.

546) I can succeed at anything I want in life no matter what.

547) I receive all the love and support I need in my life now

548) If it's not working out, I can release it with gratitude

549) Life always teaches me valuable lessons, without trying.

550) The best is yet to come or it wouldn't have come at all.

551) Today, I have the power to do anything I put my mind to.

552) We give and receive unconditional love with one another.

553) All of today's little problems fade away as time goes by.

554) Being positive feels so good that it gets me far in life.

555) Every day in every way, I'm getting better and better now

556) Everything I want comes to me easily and effortlessly now

557) Everything in my life is working out for my highest good.

558) I am willing to move forward and let go of past mistakes.

559) I deserve all the happiness in the world - no exceptions.

560) Life likes me; it wants us always to succeed together now

561) People are attracted to me as soon as I walk into a room.

562) They don't know the real me, so why should I even bother?

563) Every day in every way I am getting better and better now.

564) Every day is a new beginning and an opportunity for growth.

565) Good things happen naturally when I feel good about myself.

566) I am a magnet for wonderful relationships and experiences.

567) My mind is powerful, self-contained and extremely capable.

568) People love to be around me because of my positive nature.

569) Right now, everything in my life is working out perfectly.

570) The more ground I cover, the further my destination seems.

571) Things are always looking up for me. and better than ever.

572) Today, and all of my todays, are perfect just as they are.

573) Today is a fresh new day and I'm going to make it count.

574) Doesn't matter how bad it gets. we can always make it worse

575) Each new moment brings me an opportunity for a fresh start.

576) Every time I eat healthy food, I feel better about myself.

577) I am guided by my own inner wisdom and the love of my life.

578) I have a fantastic family that supports me unconditionally.

579) I love being with people. Their positive energy is amazing.

580) I love myself unconditionally no matter what happens today.

581) I trust that everything will work out exactly as it should.

582) Let's keep smiling because life is too short to be unhappy.

583) My success increases every day because of who I am becoming.

584) No matter what happens, everything will be okay in the end.

585) Remember that you don't have to be perfect. because nobody.

586) There is an endless supply of good vibrations headed my way.

587) Today is our day. because nobody can stop us but ourselves.

588) Today's a new beginning - I'm ready to do wonderful things.

589) Each moment is filled with peace, tranquility and happiness.

590) Every time you smile. that's one step closer to being happy.

591) Everything in my life is leading me towards my highest good.

592) I'm getting better and better at being me each and every day.

593) Life is constantly offering me lessons that I need to learn.

594) My life is really truly very happy, healthy, and successful.

595) My success increases every day because of who I am becoming.

596) No matter what happens, I will find a way to be happy today.

597) Positivity attracts positivity. and nothing can stop me now.

598) The more that I build myself up, the more I can help others.

599) There is beauty in everything and everything is beauty to me.

600) They may not say it now but they're just envying my success.

601) Today I will do one thing to move myself closer to my goals.

602) A new day has dawned and with it everything seems possible.

603) Every day is another chance for me to feel good about myself.

604) Every day is new and full of opportunities for me to succeed.

605) Every day, I learn more about myself and the world around me.

606) I've been learning a lot lately and it's exciting to know the world is so big.

607) Every day, I take the time to renew my mind, body and spirit.

608) Every moment is new beginnings and an opportunity for growth.

609) Every second is filled with nothing but pure joy and ecstasy.

610) I accept all the love the Universe has to offer me right now.

611) It doesn't matter where I am. It only matters who I've become.

612) Let them try and bring us down we'll just come back stronger.

613) Life is always working for me - and it's wonderful at it too.

614) My life is in perfect order...I don't need to force anything.

615) My smile brightens up everyone around me. even in dark times.

616) My thoughts are powerful - they will lead me to great things.

617) No matter what happens, everything will be okay in the end.

618) The best is yet to come…and it will be here before I know it.

619) They may not be able to see it yet but you are already great.

620) Today I will accomplish many things and be the best I can be.

621) Today, I am filled with gratitude for all that is in my life.

622) Today, I will do one thing to move myself closer to my goals.

623) When you expect greatness, greatness happens. Just like that.

624) Each day brings new gifts into my life. Today is no exception.

625) Everything that happens today makes me feel better and better.

626) I am deeply fulfilled by all of the amazing things in my life.

627) I am the most positive person alive. Everyone loves me for it.

628) Life is so much better when we're not afraid to love ourselves.

629) Never give up because it only gives the enemy a chance to win.

630) People look up to me because I am positive and always smiling.

631) Remember that you don't have to be perfect. because nobody is.

632) The best is yet to come. and it will be here before I know it.

633) The more love I give away, the more I have to keep for myself.

634) What a self-fulfilling prophecy. When we give love, it comes back to us in full force.

635) The only limitations in my live are the ones I set for myself.

636) The power of positive thinking will take me where I want to go

637) Today I choose happiness instead of anger. The choice is mine.

638) Today I will focus on what went right and not what went wrong.

639) Being positive attracts all kinds of great things into my life.

640) Each day I choose to be positive, things get better and better.

641) Each moment is filled with positivity. even the difficult ones.

642) Every moment brings me an opportunity for love and forgiveness.

643) Every problem has a solution. we just have to find it together.

644) Every single cell in my body is getting healthier all the time.

645) Everything always works out for everyone who TRULY wants it to.

646) The people who truly want something will always find a way to get what they desire.

647) Great things happen to me all day long when I think positively.

648) I eat what gives my body energy and vitality, every single day.

649) I have a wonderful family that loves me just the way that I am.

650) I have the power to change my life. Today will be no different.

651) I love being with people. They are drawn to my positive energy.

652) It's not what happens to us but how we react to it that matters.

653) Life isn't perfect but that doesn't mean it isn't worth living.

654) My mind sees only good things today. and they really exist too.

655) No one can keep me down for long. I bounce back up too quickly.

656) The power of positive thinking will take me where I want to go.

657) The world is always changing but what are you doing to keep up?

658) I am not what has happened to me, I am who I choose to become.

659) Today marks the beginning of becoming successful in my career.

660) "Be kind whenever possible. It is always possible." -Dalai Lama-

661) All the opportunities I need come to me easily and effortlessly.

662) Every day is an opportunity for me to grow into a better person.

663) Good health is my right, so it's only natural for me to have it.

664) I may have made mistakes before but at least I learned from them.

665) I use the power of my positive thoughts to achieve great things.

666) I will accomplish anything and everything that I put my mind to.

667) If it's not working out, it's just not meant to be at this time.

668) The more I smile, the luckier I get. Today will be no different.

669) The road may have been long but it has finally led me back home.

670) There's always a better day because the storm always blows over.

671) Today, I give myself permission to do something nice for myself.

672) Today I'll do whatever it takes to get what I want out of life.

673) As long as there is love in this world then the sky is the limit.

674) Be okay with not being okay. because the only way out is through.

675) I am getting better at everything I do - big or small - everyday.

676) I am not limited by other people's opinions, prejudices or fears.

677) Let's believe in ourselves because if we don't. no one else will.

678) Life is short so now I will live every day as if it were my last.

679) My thoughts are positive, open and receptive to all that is good.

680) Thank you, thank you, thank you, thank you, thank you, thank you.

681) The Universe brings me everything I need, exactly when I need it.

682) Today, I will be kinder to myself than anyone else could ever be.

683) We're all beautiful in our own way so never doubt yourself again.

684) You have one life, use it wisely and show what you're capable of.

685) The harder things get, the more my inner fire burns for success.

686) The world is mine to conquer today, I will take it all by storm.

687) Even if it takes a while, no matter how far I go. I'll keep going.

688) Every morning brings new opportunities for me to grow and succeed.

689) Happiness is what happens naturally when I feel good about myself.

690) It does not matter who you used to be because today we are reborn.

691) Loving others makes me feel happy inside that's what true love is.

692) My success increases with every thought, action and choice I make.

693) No who says or thinks otherwise, I am beautiful just the way I am.

694) People love being around me because of how happy I make them feel.

695) Thank you for bringing me abundance, joy, peace, good health. etc.

696) The only way out is through. So, let's work hard and never give up.

697) A smile that brings happiness to everyone around me. How wonderful.

698) I am strong enough, smart enough, and gosh darn it, people like me.

699) I have the strength to get through anything that life throws at me.

700) I take full responsibility for everything in my life - good or bad.

701) Life is so much easier when you are happy and smiling all the time.

702) Smile everyday so you can help bring joy into other people's lives.

703) The more love I give away, the more love I have to keep for myself.

704) We have a deep understanding for one another that is based on love.

705) There is nothing stopping me from achieving success except myself.

706) He doesn't know me. So why should I care about what he thinks of me?

707) I believe in myself so trust me when I say the only way to go is UP.

708) If they hurt me, then let's see how they like being ignored instead.

709) Life is so much better now that I am happy and smiling all the time.

710) Life is so much easier when you are positive and happy all the time.

711) No matter how hard things get, we'll always manage. we're survivors.

712) The Universe loves me and provides for me in amazing ways every day.

713) Today is a new beginning and I am ready to create an amazing future.

714) If you really want something in life, you have to work hard for it.

715) Always remember that you are loved and will always make a difference.

716) Being happy is easy when there are so many things to be thankful for.

717) Every moment brings with it an opportunity to do something wonderful.

718) Life loves me. Every day, in every way, I'm getting better and better.

719) My time is valuable - I spend each second doing something worthwhile.

720) No matter who says what about me - my happiness is mine & mine alone.

721) The better things I give, the better my life is.

Year 3: Positive Affirmations for Advanced Users

722) These are the best times ever. and they continue getting even better.

723) I am a strong person who is going to see this through. So, let's do it.

724) I don't have to force anything in my life...everything just works out.

725) If being confident means being conceited, then let's all be conceited.

726) It's always an uphill climb...but it's worth it when I get to the top.

727) Life is short and if I don't live it to the fullest. what's the point?

728) Life is so much better when you are positive and smiling all the time.

729) My day will go wonderfully well if I expect it too. And it starts now.

730) My inner voice guides me day & night to be the best version of myself.

731) No matter how down I feel today, I will find something to laugh about.

732) I'm a sponge for good. I soak up the energy of people who are kind, generous and helpful to me.

733) Today, I let go of all my fears and open myself to love and happiness.

734) Today I will do what needs to be done, nothing more and nothing less.

735) All of my dreams are coming true. and they start right here, right now.

736) Be kind to yourself today, for nobody knows your struggles like you do.

737) Sometimes it is hard to be kind towards yourself, but nobody knows your struggle better.

738) Life is about choices. So why don't we start making life changing ones?

739) My mind dances with good ideas and possibilities for myself and others.

740) Never let anyone break your spirit because you are stronger than words.

741) The more good that happens to me today, the more good comes back to me.

742) Today, all the lessons in my life are leading me towards self-discovery.

743) We're all beautiful in our own way. our scars are what makes us unique.

744) I love myself unconditionally for who I am no matter what happens today.

745) Every single cell in my body is getting healthier and stronger every day.

746) Good things happen when you expect them too. Today will be no different.

747) We're all unique in our own way. Our scars make us beautiful, and that's what makes them so special to see up close like this.

748) I will not be held back by anyone or anything that is trying to stop me.

749) It's okay to cry. because we all need a little 'me' time once in a while.

750) My biggest motivation is my family, they keep me going every single day.

751) The more optimistic I am, the better my life becomes. And it starts now.

752) Everything is working out in my favor and it will continue to be this way

753) I let go of everything that is not serving me, even if it brings sadness.

754) I'm not here for anyone else I'm here because my happiness depends on it.

755) It's a great day because I have found another reason to love being alive.

756) Life is always doing loving things for me, all I have to do is accept it.

757) Positive thoughts create a healthy, happy world for me and everyone else.

758) We all deserve love but most importantly. to be loved the way we want it.

759) Write down all the good things in life and watch them grow like wildfire.

760) Only good things will happen to me today and every day after this point.

761) All of my hard work has led me here today to this amazing moment in time.

762) All the best things in life come to those who work hard and never give up.

763) All the good things in my life are getting even better. and it starts now.

764) Being positive is easy because we all deserve happiness and peace in life.

765) Every moment brings with it an easy opportunity to do something wonderful.

766) Good things come to those who work for them so let's start working harder.

767) I can get anything I want by staying positive. Today will be no different.

768) It's okay to be quiet. we still love you even if you don't talk very much.

769) It's the choices you make that makes your life. So, let's choose happiness.

770) Nothing can stand in my way today because I want this more than anything.

771) Being positive fills my life with happiness and joy. It's just that simple.

772) Each moment that life gives me is an opportunity to do something wonderful.

773) Every day, I become stronger and more confident in all of my relationships.

774) Everything works out for me, so long as I have the proper attitude of mind.

775) I am determined to see the good in everything today. It's just that simple.

776) I am surrounded by people who adore me. and I feel the same way about them.

777) I'm choosing happiness over anger and negativity. Today is a new beginning.

778) I'm so glad I got this (fill in the blank) because now (List your benefits).

779) My partner loves me unconditionally no matter who I am or what I look like.

780) The more people appreciate me for being positive, the happier they make me.

781) Today is a new beginning and a blank page to write upon - so let's do this.

782) When everyone thinks I'm crazy, that's when I know I'm onto something great.

783) Every day brings me closer to better things, and today will be no different.

784) Every day, I become more loving and compassionate towards others and myself.

785) Good health comes from eating right and only the foods that nourish the body.

786) I am one step closer to success every single day - all it takes is one step.

787) I love myself more and more each day – for all the things that make me – Me.

788) It's going to be an absolutely wonderful day because who wouldn't want that?

789) Just when you think it's over, for some reason the universe has other plans.

790) Looking on the bright side gets me far in life. and nothing can stop me now.

791) No matter if they tried or not, nothing could ever stop me from being great.

792) Positivity brings me nothing but love and affection from everyone around me.

793) The more good I do for others, the better off I become. And it starts today.

794) The only way I know to live is happily, and that's exactly how it should be.

795) This day is filled with joy and happiness because being happy feels so good.

796) Today is a wonderful day that continues to get even better as it progresses.

797) Happiness is all I see. And happiness is all I want to be. And it starts now.

798) I have the power to change anything that isn't working in my life - and I do.

799) I now allow myself to receive all the good that the Universe has to offer me.

800) It's okay to feel tired sometimes. but don't let anyone tell you how to feel.

801) Life just keeps getting better and better as time goes by, and it starts now.

802) My partner mirrors my highest potential to love and be loved unconditionally.

803) The only limitations that exist in my life are those that I create for myself.

804) There's more good in this world than bad and it's time we believe that again.

805) There's no one else in the world just like me. And that's completely awesome.

806) Today I will accomplish many things because I am committed to make it happen.

807) Why should we care about what anyone has to say if they don't know us at all?

808) Every dark cloud has a silver lining so long as you continue looking for it.

809) I am beginning a brand-new chapter in my life - here's hoping it's a good one.

810) I love you more today than I did yesterday but not as much as I will tomorrow.

811) It's not about how much we give. It's about how much love we put into giving.

812) Let them have their opinions. I have my life and I'm going to start living it.

813) Let's let go of the past and learn from our mistakes because we're only human.

814) Life is constantly giving me numerous opportunities for happiness and success.

815) My past actions were good ones that helped me grow into the person I am today.

816) Success is in sight and getting closer and closer with every positive thought.

817) The more people who try to discourage me, the more determined I am to succeed.

818) The only limitations that exist in my life are those that I create for myself.

819) A smile is the cheapest way to make someone happy. let's give out more of them.

820) Everything in my life is coming up roses, and they start right here, right now.

821) It doesn't matter where I came from. All that matters is where I'm going next.

822) I have traveled all around the world, but it's time to settle down. My next stop is right here with you.

823) Life isn't always perfect but sometimes that's exactly what makes it beautiful.

824) My dreams are coming true one-by-one, each one bringing me closer to happiness.

825) My outlook on life only gets better with each breath I take. And it starts now.

826) No matter what they do or say, I'm going to continue being the best me possible.

827) Sometimes our own pride is our only obstacle. So, let's just get over ourselves.

828) The only thing I am afraid of is inaction because that's where pain comes from.

829) This is going to be a great day. and great days continue into even better ones.

830) When I feel scared or uncertain, I remind myself that everything will work out.

831) When you put a positive spin on things, that's what you attract into your life.

832) Every setback in my life allows me to become even more determined than before.

833) I go after all that I want today with no fear of failure ever holding me back.

834) Expecting the best things in life really brings them into fruition for me today.

835) I have a bright future ahead of me because I take care of myself, mind and body.

836) I love to create new things - which means I have infinite opportunities in life.

837) What we think about, we bring about. We all deserve happiness and peace in life.

838) I am beautiful. No one can make me feel the way I make myself feel, and that is something worth bragging about.

839) Mind, body, and soul are always becoming healthier and stronger every single day.

840) Success comes easily to those who are always smiling. Today will be no different.

841) Today I choose abundance over scarcity - which means there's enough for everyone.

842) Don't worry about what they think because today is my day and they're not invited.

843) I trust life will provide all that is necessary for my highest good and wellbeing.

844) My mind and body are always becoming healthier and stronger with each passing day.

845) The more good that surrounds me, the less room there is for anything bad to exist.

846) The more I smile, the luckier I get. And even better things come my way when I do.

847) We're all beautiful in our own way so never doubt yourself again for being unique.

848) We're all on the same boat. So let us always help each other out, wherever we are.

849) I will go through life like a roaring lion looking for opportunities and success.

850) Whether or not people believe in me has little to do with the reality of success.

851) No matter what happens today - I'll be okay because I choose to keep moving forward.

852) Remember your worth because it's okay to be kind to yourself every once in a while.

853) We all have our ups and downs but that's okay because it makes us who we are today.

854) We all have our ups and downs but that's okay because it makes us who we are today.

855) We all have the ability to do better. So why don't we choose to be our best selves.

856) When I breathe deeply, I expand my capacity for joy & happiness - so let's do this.

857) You know what is better than a good day? A great day. So, let's go out and have fun.

858) You will succeed in whatever you put your mind to, so let us give it our best shot.

859) Nothing will hold me back today because I am stronger than whatever holds me back.

860) Life doesn't always go your way. You will have ups and downs, but that's okay because it makes us who we are today.

861) Every breath makes me more optimistic than before, and that's just how it should be.

862) Every day is a chance for me to make positive changes and better myself as a person.

863) I have the power to change the course of my life. and I will. Today is no exception.

864) It's okay if we don't speak for a while because we'll always have that special bond.

865) Let's make every day count. because once they're gone, all that's left are memories.

866) Life starts living us the moment we start taking chances. So why don't we take them?

867) Things always work out for me because I expect them too. Today will be no different.

868) I am destined for greatness, someday everyone will see just how truly special I am.

869) Success is a journey, not a destination. I am going to enjoy every step of the way.

870) Good things happen to those who wait but better things happen to those who work hard.

871) I am happy with everything I have but I want more so today I will go after my dreams.

872) It doesn't matter what they think about my dreams. I'm going to go after them anyway.

873) Let go of anger. think of all the good times you have had with that person and smile.

874) Let's create good memories by choosing positivity because that's what really matters.

875) Life is always giving me opportunities for growth, even when it doesn't seem like it.

876) Maybe they're right. maybe I can't do it. But what does that matter if I think I can?

877) No matter what, good always overpowers evil. So, let's take that thought into our day.

878) The one who falls and gets back up is much stronger than those who never fell at all.

879) Everything that happens to me today brings with it the opportunity for many blessings.

880) I am so excited for this journey which means that I have high expectations for myself.

881) I am thankful for all the wonderful people in my life who help make it so spectacular.

882) I will never give up on myself because I'm worth it. always have been, always will be.

883) Sometimes, we feel like giving up but it's okay not to be okay because tomorrow's new.

884) The world is full of opportunities, all you have to do is look around you to see them.

885) There are always better days ahead so never give up just because things are difficult.

886) There is no such thing as 'can't' because we can do anything if we put our mind to it.

887) There is nothing better than walking along side of someone who truly loves themselves.

888) I can overcome any obstacle if I believe in myself, take action, and refuse to give up.

889) In every relationship, we both lovingly put each other first above everyone else always.

890) It is an honor to be here today but tomorrow is a new day so let's make the most of it.

891) Just breathe. remember your worth and let's make each other feel like we're all enough.

892) Life becomes easier when you expect great things to happen. Today will be no different.

893) Success comes easily when I stay positive and always look on the bright side of things.

894) The best of times is when I am around people who appreciate me for my positive nature.

895) When life takes you on a bumpy ride. hold onto your seat because it always gets better.

896) I have the key to success today so I'm going to turn that key and unlock my potential.

897) Every experience is an opportunity for me to learn something new about myself or others.

898) Let's spread the love because when we do, everything else just seems to fall into place.

899) Maybe being happy isn't the best thing in life but it's definitely worth all the effort.

900) Success is mine to have, so long as I feel good right now. Which I do, every single day.

901) Successful people are always smiling and looking at the bright side of things. So can I.

902) Wherever I am right now is exactly where I need to be - even if it doesn't seem like it.

903) While others may judge us. it doesn't mean they are entitled to our happiness or success.

904) I am a strong person who can accomplish anything as long as they believe in themselves.

905) Life is full of opportunities, I'm going to grab them by the handfuls and change my life.

906) Life is simple. Whenever I stop over-thinking things, everything always works out for me.

907) Perfection is boring. So why don't we forget about it and start celebrating our mistakes?

908) Success comes easily when I am positive because positivity attracts success into my life.

909) The best thing about every minute of every day is that there are 60 of them in each hour.

910) Today is a new day - so let's get rid of any negativity & fill our lives with positivity.

911) Today is a new day. So, let's take control of our lives, stop reacting and start creating.

912) Today, I am focusing on my happiness because refuse to make myself believe any different.

913) Every day is an opportunity to become stronger, wiser, braver, and more successful then.

914) My success rate increases every day. I learn from my mistakes and they do not define me.

915) When one door closes another door opens; each new opportunity brings with it fresh hope.

916) Being alone doesn't mean being lonely. as long as you have your mind, anything is possible.

917) I don't need to find any more excuses. I can overcome anything I set my mind to achieving.

918) If we can't learn to embrace our differences, how will we ever be able to live in harmony?

919) In my relationships, I allow myself to be selfishly cherished as much as I cherish others.

920) It doesn't matter who said something negative about you because in the end, they're wrong.

921) Life isn't about waiting for the storm to pass...it's about learning to dance in the rain.

922) Life just keeps getting better and better as time goes by, and today will be no different.

923) Optimistic people are always happy and smiling. Today I'm going to be one of those people.

924) Out of all the things we could worry about, why not choose to leave those worries behind?

925) The more love & light I bring into my life, the more beauty & abundance I attract into it.

926) The only way out is through. So, stay positive and keep pushing no matter how hard it gets.

927) Today is an amazing day to be alive today. (Why?) Because it's up to me that this is true.

928) Everything that happens now benefits me in some way, no matter how difficult it may seem.

929) No matter where I end up, I know that I will succeed because there's nobody else like me.

930) Every breath I take brings me closer to greatness. and not just in my mind. But in reality.

931) Everything that happens to me today gives me an opportunity to grow and be a better person.

932) I am divinely guided throughout each and every day by my heart which never steers me wrong.

933) I am kinder to myself than anyone else will ever be - which is why I am my own best friend.

934) I am more than capable of achieving my goals and dreams - I just have to believe in myself.

935) It's all working out for my highest good. If it's not, then it's an opportunity for growth.

936) Never let anyone dull your sparkle because you are unique and amazing just the way you are.

937) There is plenty of time left in the day to do what needs doing - no need to hurry or worry.

938) When you think positively, you attract positive things into your life. It works every time.

939) You are strong enough to get past the bad things in life so keep pushing until you succeed.

940) You are strong enough to get past the bad things in life so keep pushing until you succeed.

941) My dreams will become a reality because anything is possible with hard work and dedication.

942) Always try your best because life isn't about winning or losing, it's how you play the game.

943) Always try your best because life isn't about winning or losing, it's how you play the game.

944) I love you to the moon and back. and I never want to hear that you aren't good enough again.

945) Let's encourage other people because everyone needs a boost now and then to keep them going.

946) Let's start believing in ourselves because if other people don't believe then why should we?

947) My inner peace and happiness grow with each day that I am able to move past any negativity.

948) My right path will reveal itself in its own time, but patience makes my heart grow stronger.

949) No matter who we are or where we come from. The best thing we can do is believe in ourselves.

950) Optimism is the key to getting everything you want out of life. It's easy once you know how.

951) Today is a new start and a fresh beginning, all the best things in life are within my reach.

952) We don't decide who lives or dies. So, let's try to make every day count as if it's our last.

953) We might be having a bad day today but remember that everything will look up again tomorrow.

954) When we try, we reach our destination. So let us never give up because there is always hope.

955) My motivation and dedication make me unstoppable as I continue on this journey to success.

956) My past only defines me if I allow it to hold me back from what lies ahead of me right now.

957) Each new moment brings me an opportunity to let go of the past and move forward with my life.

958) Every brings with it an easy opportunity to improve myself, others, and this world around me.

959) I can't wait for the wonderful things life has in store for me today. It's going to be great.

960) I don't care how many times I fall down in life as long as each time I get back up with ease.

961) If we all had a little more empathy in our lives there would be a lot less fighting going on.

962) If you don't like something about yourself. change it.. But never forget where you came from.

963) In every relationship, we both do everything we can to make sure that our love lasts forever.

964) Keep your mind open to new things and possibilities because you never know what might happen.

965) Let go of whatever holds us back or weighs us down because only then, will we be able to fly.

966) Let's not be afraid to open our hearts today because no matter what, life is always worth it.

967) Loving myself helps me to be confident in my own skin showing others who love themselves too.

968) My home is my safe haven; it's where I find my peace, comfort and most importantly, my heart.

969) The things I need are already within me so why do I keep looking for them outside of myself?

970) There are plenty of new opportunities available to me right now that will benefit me greatly.

971) If you want something, work hard for it and nothing will stop you from achieving your goals.

972) Being optimistic gets me what I want out of each moment. And right now, I want to be positive.

973) I don't need to be afraid of the future because as long as today is going well, then I'm happy.

974) Let's stop worrying about what other people might think of us because they're never satisfied.

975) My relationships are long lasting, passionate, harmonious, loving, kind, romantic and sensual.

976) No matter how far away you are. I will always find a way to get back to you That is a promise.

977) Remember that everything happens for a reason and every bad experience only makes us stronger.

978) Take some risks today even if they seem scary. You won't know your limits until you push them.

979) What comes around goes around so let's have positive outlook and be the change we wish to see.

980) I'm burning through life like a firework. All of my hard work is going to pay off in the end.

981) I am a beautiful & unique creation, exactly as I'm supposed to be - who I'd always meant to be.

982) I follow my heart's desires which always lead me towards happiness, joy, peace and fulfillment.

983) I'm not going to be everyone's cup of tea but I can guarantee that they're not my flavor either

984) It only takes a little push to turn the world right side up. So, keep pushing until you succeed.

985) It's okay not to be okay but even better when you can turn it around with a smile on your face.

986) Let us not focus on all the bad things in life and instead, let's concentrate on the good ones.

987) Our minds will always wonder but let's push the negativity out and focus on positivity instead.

988) The easiest way to make it through the difficult times in my life is with positive affirmations.

989) The more positive I get, the more successful my life becomes. And that's just how it should be.

990) Sometimes we have to fall down in order to get up again with the knowledge we need to succeed.

991) Don't be afraid of the future because you have control over your life so make it a positive one.

992) Even when I'm in a bad mood, there is no way I can't find at least one reason to be happy today.

993) I now choose to let go of my worries and trust that everything is working out the way it should.

994) It's okay if things don't turn out the way I planned today. At least something new will happen.

995) It's okay if you're scared, we all are but what makes us different is that we keep going anyways.

996) It's okay not to be okay. but even better when you can turn it around with a smile on your face.

997) It's okay not to be okay. but even better when you can turn it around with a smile on your face.

998) Let's embrace our uniqueness because we were born to stand out. So, let's be ourselves and shine.

999) Let's learn from our mistakes instead of dwelling on them so we can become better people for it.

1000) No one can ever take away my happiness because it isn't theirs to take. it belongs solely to me.

1001) The most important thing in my life is always feeling fantastic. And I feel fantastic right now.

1002) The power of positive thinking is strong; manifesting abundance into my life rapidly and easily.

1003) Today you will become the best version of yourself. you know why? Because you are working on it.

1004) "The only person you should try to be better than, is the person you were yesterday." -Anonymous-

1005) Every day brings with it an easy opportunity to improve myself, others, and this world around me.

1006) Everything always works out in the end & if it hasn't worked out yet then maybe it's not the end.

1007) How we feel is a choice. So why don't we choose happiness instead of feeling sorry for ourselves.

1008) Life may be difficult at times but that doesn't mean that this journey is impossible to overcome.

1009) Remember, every day you spend upset is a waste of happiness so let's embrace positivity every day.

1010) There is evil everywhere but there is also good. So, let's focus on the good and not give up hope.

1011) You deserve love, happiness, and the best life has to offer. So always be kind to yourself first.

1012) All it takes is one simple shift of perspective for me to have a drastically more positive life.

1013) Every moment I am more optimistic than ever before means success is just a heartbeat away from me.

1014) Every single day that passes brings us one step closer to our dreams and goals so let's work hard.

1015) I know that I am going places so let's go together. I'll guide the way if you just follow my lead.

1016) I see the best in everyone and everything around me because I know that's where my abundance lies.

1017) It's all working out for me and not someone else. If it's not, then it's an opportunity for growth.

1018) It's okay to have a bad day. we all have them and tomorrow is another chance for us to get better.

1019) No matter where I go or who I meet, in the end everything I want in life can only come from within.

1020) Once again I am able to get through another tough day because I know tomorrow will be even better.

1021) The past cannot control me anymore because I'm in the process of becoming who I really want to be.

1022) Today will be a great day no matter what happens because my life has been full of greatness so far.

1023) We're not afraid of anything. if we believe in ourselves after everything life has put us through.

1024) I can do anything if I put my mind to it, so let's go out there and show them what we're made of.

1025) Each day that I wake up breathing gives me a reason to smile. So, smile with me for waking up alive.

1026) I don't always know what's going on but that's okay because without darkness there can be no light.

1027) I now forgive those who have hurt me in the past, as I have now forgiven myself for hurting others.

1028) If someone makes a mistake then we should always be the first ones to forgive them because we would.

1029) It's all working out for me and not someone else. If it's not, then it's an opportunity for growth.

1030) It's going to be a wonderful day filled with laughter, smiles and happiness. Just because I say so.

1031) Making mistakes doesn't make me less of who I am. It makes me more of an infinitely evolving being.

1032) No one knows how long they'll be on this planet so we should live each and every day to its fullest.

1033) No one knows how long they'll be on this planet so we should live each and every day to its fullest.

1034) Sometimes we forget. it's not about how much money we make, it's about how much we enjoy our lives.

1035) There is always light at the end of the tunnel so we should never give up and look for it each day.

1036) Today I am thankful for all that I have accomplished and for what I will accomplish in the future.

1037) Today marks the beginning of a new chapter, where I am going to be living my life with no regrets.

1038) It's not what they say but how it makes me feel so why should I care about anything besides myself?

1039) Make today count because tomorrow may never come. Do what you love and spend time with the people who matter most in your life, for they are needed more than ever before.

1040) The things I believe in are mine alone so why should I care if someone else tries to take them away?

1041) Success is getting to the point where everything is going right because that's how living should be.

1042) The more people appreciate me for being so happy and smiling all the time, the happier they make me.

1043) The only thing worth worrying about is whether or not your soul is capable of loving unconditionally

1044) Let's make today count because tomorrow isn't promised so never forget to do what you love each day.

1045) Today is a new day. let go of yesterday and believe that today will bring wonderful things your way.

1046) I am the master of my destiny so whatever happens today is exactly what's supposed to be happening.

1047) Today marks the beginning of a new chapter in my life where everything is going to fall into place.

1048) Each day gets better than its predecessor because I am trying harder than ever before to be positive.

1049) Every day is a new day to get better & better at whatever it is I am working on - I will not give up.

1050) Every day that passes brings me closer to the greatness that each day brings. Today is no exception.

1051) Always think before you speak because not only will it show class but respect for yourself and others.

1052) Every mistake makes us wiser- so why not make a few mistakes (big ones even) because they're worth it.

1053) I'll never be perfect. but that doesn't mean I can't show everyone how amazing "imperfections" can be.

1054) Life is a journey- so why not stop worrying about the destination and focus on the beauty of the road?

1055) Failure is not an option today because I am too strong of a person to let failure get the best of me.

1056) A new day brings with it infinite possibilities of how amazing this day could go if I choose happiness.

1057) Be grateful for what you have because some people don't even have half of what we've been blessed with.

1058) Behind every great man is a greater woman and remember ladies, there is nothing wrong with being single.

1059) Each moment of the day I spend in a state of happiness and positivity brings joy to everyone around me.

1060) The only person who can rescue me is me. So today let's work together to escape the hells of our minds.

1061) You can do anything if you put your mind to it, so let's go out there and show them what we're made of.

1062) Today is a new day where anything can happen. Anything that does happen will be something good though.

1063) Don't ever let someone become a habit because that's all they'll ever be. just something you used to do.

1064) Every day gets better than its predecessor because looking on the bright side is easier than ever before.

1065) Every moment brings me closer to success because thinking positively does that for me. It's that simple.

1066) I have all the tools I need within me to become who I desire to be. I am more than enough, just as I am.

1067) I have the power to choose whatever I want to experience in my life - which means I can choose anything.

1068) I trust myself enough to know that if today were my last day on earth I would die happy with no regrets.

1069) If I make a mistake, I will dust myself off and keep moving forward no matter how difficult it may seem.

1070) I'm right where I'm supposed to be: in this moment, in this day, doing what I love and loving what I do.

1071) No one is perfect because everyone has flaws but one day you will find someone who loves your flaws too.

1072) Sometimes it doesn't matter if you're right or wrong because all that matters is your belief in yourself

1073) Sometimes people leave without a reason just remember that sometimes they come back without a reason too.

1074) Sometimes people treat us like a book that has no ending. but the truth is that we determine how it ends.

1075) We only fail when we give up on ourselves. but why don't we make today the day we stop all self-sabotage.

1076) As long as we live in peace, stay positive and focus on what we want, then all our dreams will come true.

Year 4: Long Positive Affirmations for Experts

1077) Don't waste your time on people who don't value what you bring to the table because they're not worth it.

1078) Greatness is just a thought away, which means today will be great just like tomorrow will be even greater.

1079) Having a positive attitude brings all kinds of wonderful things into my life. Everything in every moment.

1080) I accept that what is, is and stand in gratitude as it unfolds into something better than I had imagined.

1081) I know exactly what direction I need to take to get where I want to be so let's take a moment and decide.

1082) Remember to take care of yourself before you can take care for others. that's how the saying goes, right?

1083) There are so many positive things happening right now that anything bad seems impossible to even conceive

1084) We all have good days and bad days. but why not learn from the latter so we can enjoy more of our former?

1085) Every day that goes by where all that happens are good things is another step towards reaching my dreams.

1086) Today is full of opportunities for me to succeed and accomplish the goals that I want to make a reality.

1087) Be grateful for the little things in life because they go away quickly, not knowing how special they were.

1088) Don't worry about what others think or say because the only thing that matters is what you think and feel.

1089) Every day that goes by makes me more aware of what really matters most in my life. And that's being happy.

1090) Getting it right the first time is extremely rare but if we try again and again eventually it will happen.

1091) If a problem has a solution, there's nothing to worry about. If it doesn't, worrying won't solve anything.

1092) It doesn't matter how many times I fall down in life because all that matters is that I get back up again.

1093) It takes one good thought to wipe out another bad one so let's concentrate on the positive things in life.

1094) It's normal to make mistakes in life. we all do. But what matters most is how we learn from them and grow.

1095) No matter what they do and say, I will always be me and you know what? I'm happy with who I am. I like me.

1096) They may say that everyone's entitled to their own opinion but that doesn't mean I have to listen to them.

1097) The amount of positivity I have in my life is in direct correlation to how happy I feel on a daily basis.

1098) If I listen closely enough, I can hear only my heart beating. That is how close we are and always will be.

1099) If we don't like how things are going then we have to change them and that is exactly what I'm going to do.

1100) Life is a journey and not a destination which means try your best to have fun during this ride called life.

1101) Life isn't always easy so when hard times come around. let's not forget that it will eventually get better.

1102) Sunshine and rainbows. that's all I see when my mind is in a positive state of being. And it feels so good.

1103) The only person who can stop me winning big in life are myself so let's not even give them the opportunity.

1104) Today I will trust life. even in my toughest moments and it will be the best decision I've made in a while.

1105) When you love yourself then that's when you'll find true happiness. So, until then, love me unconditionally.

1106) You don't need anybody but yourself. you were strong before you met them and will be stronger without them.

1107) All that it takes for me right now is one positive thought to change the direction of the rest of my life.

1108) I know what it takes to be successful, now I'm simply taking the steps necessary towards making it happen.

1109) My positive thoughts lead to positive actions which allow me to become more successful each and every day.

1110) Every day gets better than its predecessor because I am trying harder than ever to be positive all the time.

1111) Every day is better than the next because that's how life works when you expect positive outcomes. And I do.

1112) If you're sad, think about all the things that make you happy and remember there is still good in the world.

1113) I'm not afraid of anything or anyone in this world because there is nothing or no one here that can hurt me.

1114) My mother is very proud of me & can see how successful I have become - just by taking small steps at a time.

1115) I love the way life works. When I do something selfless, good things happen to me.

1116) There is no need to go searching for happiness when it's going to find me anyways. You can trust me on this.

1117) Every second, minute, hour, day that I put in the work is time that brings me closer to where I want to be.

1118) Everything happens for a reason. No matter what happens remember that it's always possible to be happy today.

1119) If letting them walk all over me gets the happiness I want, then why shouldn't I let them think they've won?

1120) If this has taught us anything, it's that nothing lasts forever so why don't we enjoy the ride while it does?

1121) Knowing myself allows me to be perfectly comfortable in my own skin showing others who loving themselves too.

1122) Remember the past only makes us stronger because it shows our growth which allows us to move forward feeling.

1123) Success feels very good, and success is on my side today because of the way I think about everything in life.

1124) The next step in making my dreams come true is simply believing they will - so why not start believing today?

1125) There is no need to go searching for happiness when it's going to find you anyways. You can trust me on this.

1126) There is nothing wrong with making mistakes as long as we learn from them and become better and wiser for it.

1127) Everyday listen and talk to people who lift your spirits up because then their positivity will inspire us too.

1128) I am not here by accident, I am made for this world. So, let's get out there and show what makes us so special.

1129) I am the only one who can help myself so I must be strong enough to face my fears and not give up on anything.

1130) I can't go wrong with being so happy all the time because happiness only attracts more happiness into my life.

1131) I was made to achieve greatness, damn it. So, let's get out there and get what should have been mine all along.

1132) I'm trying my best not to hate you because after all, there is nothing fair in war so let me just say goodbye.

1133) Positivity attracts even more positivity into your life. A great thing when you expect great things to happen.

1134) Self-doubt will always try to enter our minds but we can't let it because believing in ourselves is important.

1135) Today, let's not worry about what people are going to say or think about us because life is too short to care.

1136) We can do anything we set our minds to so let's blaze the trails and create the future that everyone deserves.

1137) You should never make your happiness dependent on other people because we all know that they're unpredictable.

1138) All it takes is one big break for everything to fall into place. I am patiently waiting for my break to come.

1139) Just because I say it now. doesn't mean it's true. So, let's make today the day we start believing in ourselves.

1140) The only way to fail, is to stop trying which means you should stay motivated for at least as long as it takes.

1141) Today I am a hard-working, determined, and passionate person who deserves to live a happy and fulfilling life.

1142) I am not letting anybody else take away my happiness so let's support each other to build an empire out of dust.

1143) I know a good day when I see one, and that's exactly what today is going to be filled with from start to finish.

1144) I know a great day is only a thought away, and that thought leads into reality. And did it work? You bet it did.

1145) I know what I've been through in life but instead of letting it hold me back, today i'll let it push me forward.

1146) It's okay if some people don't understand or appreciate what I do, I'm on my own path & I can't please everyone.

1147) Let's celebrate everything we achieve and never feel bad for being a kind person. We all have a purpose in life.

1148) Let's not worry about what other people think of us. because they're too busy worrying about their life anyways.

1149) Never judge anyone because there are only two things that they can do. either let it go or hold onto it forever.

1150) We always have a choice so today let's choose to love ourselves for who we are instead of putting ourselves last.

1151) Positivity is a good thing. And that's exactly how I feel today, which means success is right around the corner.

1152) To-day will let go of my past and simply focus on making the most of my present because it's all about progress.

1153) You never know what someone is going through, so you should always be patient. There are only two options for them -letting go or holding on too tightly.

1154) When things are tough don't give up because there is light at the end of the road. You can make it through this.

1155) Each day I feel a little better about myself and each day I learn something new to improve myself even further.

1156) Don't let anyone steal your dreams because you're the one who has control over your own life. So, make it special.

1157) If they don't want to be a part of your life let them miss out. We were never meant to be anyone's second choice.

1158) It doesn't matter how many mistakes we make, as long as we keep trying new things, the possibilities are endless.

1159) My past is behind me. which means today is all about growth and betterment. Let's make this day count, shall we?

1160) There is beauty in everything if we make the choice to embrace it. So, let's start embracing the beauty around us.

1161) Trying is the first step towards failure so if you really want something, stop making excuses and just go for it.

1162) Each moment in time brings me closer to happiness and success because I have a positive mind set about everything.

1163) I won't let other people's opinions cloud how I feel about myself which means I can be happy for no reason at all.

1164) It's okay not to be okay sometimes so lay down your burdens because you don't have to carry them every single day.

1165) People are here today and gone tomorrow which means we need to make the most out of every opportunity given to us.

1166) Some people may want to see me fall but I know that the way to rise is simply to keep on standing. So, let's do it.

1167) Some people think that my beliefs are crazy, we'll let them laugh at me while I'm laughing all the way to the bank.

1168) Sometimes great things take time. but time is one thing this universe has plenty of, so there's no reason to rush.

1169) We all complain sometimes but tomorrow is a new day so why don't we focus on the positive instead of the negative?

1170) Why should we bother worrying about what other people think? All that matters is how good we feel about ourselves.

1171) Every minute is an opportunity to make a good impression which means you should always keep your chin up and smile.

1172) If life gets too much then take a few minutes for yourself to relax. you deserve it so don't ever forget that okay?

1173) It might sound crazy but we are all superheroes. So, let's focus on our strengths and use them to help other people.

1174) Laughter is the best medicine so let's give each other a break, celebrate our differences & learn from one another.

1175) Let us remember that there is someone out there who cares and is willing to help without asking anything in return.

1176) Life is precious and we should make the most of it. Let's challenge ourselves to do more good things with our life.

1177) I am at peace with where I currently am in life, knowing that I will continue growing & expanding into new horizons.

1178) It's okay to go off the beaten path. because sometimes, we have to get lost in order to find a better way back home.

1179) Nothing is permanent in this world except change itself - and when the time is right, all change will happen for me.

1180) When others judge me, it only reflects their own insecurities & ignorance because they are so much alike themselves.

1181) If you want something, you have to do whatever it takes to achieve greatness. Success comes from actions not words.

1182) All my relationships are mutually beneficial & positively impactful for all involved - because that's what I deserve.

1183) Every person has their own unique thoughts & feelings which means that everyone's truth is different - not just mine.

1184) I am the leader of my own life and it is up to me to choose what I want to do with it. So, let's get moving, shall we?

1185) I hope you know that no matter what happens, I truly care about your wellbeing. You will always have a friend in me.

1186) I to waste another second feeling sorry for myself because this is my life and I am going to make the best out of it.

1187) Sometimes we forget that we are not alone. I'm here with you always and forever no matter if we're together or apart.

1188) There are plenty of things about this world that aren't fair. but why waste time complaining when we can take action?

1189) Who cares if they don't like me. I'll keep being fabulous & eventually they'll have no choice but to see what you see.

1190) No matter what, I will keep moving forward with the belief that success is inevitable. There's no stopping me today.

1191) Every problem I face has the potential to become a blessing in disguise - even if it doesn't seem like that right now.

1192) Everyone makes mistakes from time to time but what matters most is that I own up to them, learn from them and move on.

1193) I believe that everything is working out for me and not someone else. If it's not, then it's an opportunity for growth.

1194) I believe that you can do anything if you put your mind to it, so let's go out there and show them what we're made of.

1195) I have infinite potential to change my life in any way I choose - because this moment is not the only one that exists.

1196) I will let you go because it's the only way I can survive. I love you but it kills me inside knowing that your near me.

1197) I've learned from my past and grown into a better person, now it's time to take action and get out of my comfort zone.

1198) Let's not focus on negativity because we can create our own destiny. We all deserve happiness, peace and love in life.

1199) Let's focus less on what happened yesterday and more on what we're going to do tomorrow. So, let's make it a great one.

1200) I am always changing. Every day is another opportunity to shape my life the way that best suits me and no moment should be more sacred than any other because there are infinite possibilities out there for us all.

1201) Positivity leads to success, which leads to me being even more optimistic in every moment. Today will be no different.

1202) Remember the past only makes us stronger because it shows our growth which allows us to move forward feeling positive.

1203) The present belongs to me so I will live my life how I want to. I have goals and the determination to accomplish them.

1204) Today, and always, my partner can think of nothing else but showing me endless affection in every single way possible.

1205) We all have a choice so always choose happiness and positivity because it will make your life so much more meaningful.

1206) We are all unique. Just like a snowflake. Each one of us is different yet beautiful in our own way, so celebrate that.

1207) You have no idea how strong you are until being strong is the only choice you have left. So, let's make today that day.

1208) Expecting greatness in every moment makes it come into fruition for me in every moment. That's the power of positivity.

1209) I am talented & I'm not afraid to show everyone what I can do. There's no time like today to start living your dreams.

1210) I never give up on my dreams because I know that if I can see them through, then success will come knocking at my door.

1211) I want success but I won't settle until I get exactly what I deserve and that is the only way that we will all succeed.

1212) I will not let yesterday's disappointments control my today because sometimes the greatest steps are taken in the dark.

1213) Let's not focus on negativity because we can create our own destiny. We all deserve happiness, peace and love in life.

1214) We all have different paths which means let's not compare ourselves to others because everyone is on their own journey.

1215) We can't change what we can't see. So, let's stop thinking about what we don't want and start focusing on the life we do.

1216) You create your own luck by being positive and believing in yourself which makes you unstoppable. So never forget that.

1217) Push yourself harder than anyone else because one day you will wake up and see that life is passing you by. Then what?

1218) Don't be afraid of change because if you don't like something in your life. you always have the power to make it better.

1219) Don't be afraid of what people will think or say about you. Be yourself and if they don't like it. that's their problem.

1220) Life isn't perfect it's just perfectly what we make of it. We all deserve to be happy and live a life filled with peace.

1221) Pain is temporary but if we're ever feeling sad, remember that life is really just a game and you can always play again.

1222) Positivity leads to more positivity which leads into greatness, and that's just how it works. So, bring on the greatness.

1223) They're just words and words are meant for change So why don't we make today the day where things start changing for us?

1224) We've all heard "no" a couple times in our lives but what do they know anyway? We were born to win so let's do our best.

1225) I am not afraid of success because I know what hard work can do for me. So, let's get out there and make something happen.

1226) I will feel good about life every second of the day. Why wouldn't I when I have so much to be happy about in this moment?

1227) Today will be filled with happiness and positivity no matter what happens. Because that's how I choose to think about it.

1228) We are all our own hero's and the only person that can stop us from being great is ourselves, so why don't we be greater?

1229) We both fully trust each other with our hearts as we share our dreams with one another making them all come true together.

1230) We can do anything if we believe in ourselves. So, let's go out there, conquer the world and show them what we're made of.

1231) Before you can look back on your life with pride you must first learn to walk forward without regret. So, let's start now.

1232) Every breath I take gets me closer to the greatness that's going to happen in my life today. It just keeps getting better.

1233) I just cannot wait for the day that I have paid my dues in life because it's going to be a glorious day when that happens.

1234) I pray today, not to complain about my situation. but to keep learning from it until one day I can finally say " I made it".

1235) If you want something then do whatever it takes to get it & remember. it's worth every ounce of effort you put towards it.

1236) It doesn't matter what kind of day someone else is having. I always expect great things in my life to happen. And they do.

1237) It doesn't matter what someone else does. my life only keeps getting more positive. And why would I want it any other way?

1238) It's all working out for me and not someone else. If it's not, then it's an opportunity for growth. I deserve to be happy.

1239) Let's make sure our dreams are clear and want we truly desire so no matter what happens in life we know what we want most.

1240) Life is unpredictable. but if we can accept that, then why don't we stop letting it scare us and start taking more risks?

1241) Positivity attracts even more positivity, and it's something I'm grateful for because it's what makes everything so great.

1242) Positivity is one of the most powerful things in the universe because if we fill our minds with good things, good happens.

1243) Sometimes it's okay to break down because it's a chance for us to think about our lives and fix the parts that are broken.

1244) This might be challenging but if we want something bad enough then nothing will stand in our way. Let's prove them wrong.

1245) When times are tough don't give up because it will get better. The sun rises everyday, a new beginning for us to start over.

1246) All of my past experiences have made me better, wiser and stronger - so I am prepared for anything that comes my way today.

1247) Be strong and always remember that you're not alone because somewhere out there, someone is feeling exactly the way you do.

1248) It's okay for me to feel a little overwhelmed in life because that's when I know it's time to take a step back and reflect.

1249) Positivity breeds positivity which leads into greatness which leads to even more happiness. Who wouldn't want that? Not me.

1250) The only reason I know that I can do something is because it hasn't been done before so let's show them what we're made of.

1251) We might be having a bad day but there's someone out there who has it worse. Remember to be grateful for what you have now.

1252) When someone is cruel to us, remember to ignore them and walk away with your head held. Bet they won't mess with you again.

1253) Whenever you feel lonely. I hope you remember that there is someone out there who cares and is willing to be there for you.

1254) You can't pick and choose who is going to love you. but somehow, when you least expect it, the best person will come along.

1255) At this very moment, all is at peace as everything falls into place as it should. So, let's appreciate it as we push forward.

1256) I don't have time for the people who want to bring me down because I am too busy watching my vision come together as I plan.

1257) My focus today is on thinking good thoughts because my words & actions will always follow the direction my thoughts take me.

1258) Problems don't live in my mind - they live in my body. So, let's get moving & start getting rid of all the negativity inside.

1259) Remember, we are only human so if we make mistakes today. give us a second chance to make it right because nobody's perfect.

1260) We all experience challenges but it's how we deal with them that matters which means let's take a deep breath and stay calm.

1261) We all have our own battles to fight so let us in turn, help someone else in need in order to make the world a kinder place.

1262) Each & every day is a brand-new opportunity to take my life into my own hands, choose what I want to experience and have fun.

1263) Every negative thought acts like a drop of poison in my mind, but every positive thought acts like pure medicine for my soul.

1264) I am beautiful just the way I am, nobody has the right to change me because they're only changing their perception of beauty.

1265) I have a lot to look forward to today and every day because of my constant positivity. And why would I want it any other way?

1266) I know that eventually there will be someone who will see my value just like I see it but until then, let me shine on my own.

1267) Knowing the best things in life are on their way makes me feel great about today before it even starts. Well, why wouldn't I?

1268) Let's stop worrying so much about what other people think of us. because they're too busy worrying about their lives anyways.

1269) Sometimes people think that our dreams are bigger than we are but trust me on this, not a single star ever fell from the sky.

1270) Stop worrying about what people think about you, because their opinion is irrelevant. It's not worth your time at all.

1271) Today and every day we have the opportunity to be someone better than who we were yesterday. Let's take full advantage of it.

1272) When life gets busy, remember to stop for a second and appreciate the simple things because they are what make us who we are.

1273) Don't be afraid to laugh because every day won't be good all the time but we need to know when to smile even during hard times.

1274) Every day gets better than the next because that's how time works when you think positively. And that's just how it should be.

1275) Every moment in life is like a new chapter - meaning I can be whatever I want to be with hard work, perseverance & dedication.

1276) Everyone makes mistakes from time to time but what matters most is how we learn from them, grow from them & move on from them.

1277) Getting up after falling is hard but staying down is harder. Let's just pick ourselves up and move on with our lives, shall we?

1278) If you want your dreams to come true, then wake up early every single morning because that is when they do most of their work.

1279) Remember that nobody is perfect so instead of looking at your reflection in comparison to others, cherish how far you've come.

1280) Sometimes people think they can get over on you but you have to show them that they can't. So, let's prove these people wrong.

1281) The waters might look deep but if we trust ourselves, then there is no way to fail. So, let's dive right in and start swimming.

1282) The world keeps throwing us lemons so there is no time like the present to make some damn good lemonade. Let's make it happen.

1283) Today I will expect greatness from each and every moment because positivity attracts greatness into my life. It's that simple.

1284) Today, and always, life fits us perfectly, like two pieces of a puzzle coming together as one because that's what true love is.

1285) We all make mistakes but remember not to dwell on them because there will always be a brighter future ahead for us. Just look.

1286) We need to be reminded that you can always bounce back up when nothing seems to go your way because life is full of surprises.

1287) We're all beautiful in our own way so never doubt yourself again for being unique. because that's what makes us special today.

1288) We're all different in our own way so never doubt yourself again for being unique. because that's what makes us special today.

1289) Don't worry about it because there are always going to be bad days but that doesn't mean that we have to stay sad all the time.

1290) Every moment in my life is a positive one because I'm so optimistic about everything in life. And that's just how it should be.

1291) It doesn't matter what situation you're going through, I hope you know that I am here for you and I care about your wellbeing.

1292) Let's not give up on our dreams. Instead let's learn from every mistake. When things get tough, know that this too shall pass.

1293) Talk to someone you trust because sometimes talking things out releases tension and lets us see a better side of the situation.

1294) Wherever you are, whatever you do. just remember that life is too short for us to spend most of it feeling sorry for ourselves.

1295) Be kind to others because everyone is fighting a hard battle that we know nothing about and forgiveness is always the way to go.

1296) If there's someone you care about. consider giving them just one call because they need to know they're not alone in this world.

1297) Let's focus on inner beauty by being kind to everyone we come in contact with. Because it's easy to be mean but hard to be kind.

1298) Some people are blessed with opportunities, I'm blessed with endless opportunities. So why shouldn't it be me who fulfills them?

1299) The best part about today are the many positive things that are waiting ahead for me to think about them. So that's what I'll do.

1300) The best things in life always come to those who are positive about what they want in this moment. And that's just how it works.

1301) There are tons of opportunities in this world if we make sure to look for them instead of assuming they will never come our way.

1302) They can laugh all they want because tomorrow is another day and you know what happens to those who laugh last? They laugh best.

1303) I hope you know that today and every day after no matter what happens, I want you to remember something. I care about you deeply.

1304) Life keeps getting better and better, day by day. And that's all I want out of life so why would I want it any other way?

1305) Positivity breeds positivity which brings about an even greater feeling of joy than before. And why wouldn't I want that?

1306) The best part about life is that it keeps getting better and better with every day that passes. That's what makes today exciting.

1307) There may be other options out there but there is always going to be one option for me and that would be success. So, bring it on.

1308) When one door closes another opens; new opportunities are always around the corner. I welcome change with open arms into my life.

1309) When you feel good now, it'll be easier than ever before to just keep feeling good as time goes on. Who would've thought?

1310) Why should I give anyone else the power to tell me how I'm supposed to live my life? It's mine so let's go out there and live it.

1311) You are special for not being like everyone else which means we're all unique and we should embrace that instead of degrading it.

1312) Every day in life brings something new and exciting just waiting for me to experience it firsthand. Can you believe that?

1313) Every day is a new beginning so it's not the end of the world if things don't go my way just as long as I find a way that they do.

1314) I am grateful for everything that's happened in my life - even the mistakes & lessons because they helped me get where I am today.

1315) I don't know why he is doing this. but I do know that things will work out because they always do. You just have to keep believing.

1316) I don't need to make sense. I just need to feel good. So why don't we choose happiness instead of making excuses not to be happy?

1317) It doesn't matter how many times you've failed. all that matters is failing forward which means trying again instead of giving up.

1318) It's okay to fail because it makes us strong if we learn from our mistakes. But the only person who fails is the one who gives up.

1319) Let's look at all of the positive things in our lives because it is only going to make us more appreciative. So, let's be grateful.

1320) Let's not tell lies to ourselves. no matter what we deserve happiness just like everyone else does, so let's start by being honest.

1321) Let's stop wishing for other people to change because maybe, they were put in this world to teach us how to love unconditionally.

1322) My mistakes don't define me. But they do help shape my future so let's not get it twisted here. Everything happens for a reason.

1323) Sometimes you have to ignore people if they can't understand what matters most. us. So, let's be better than them and move forward.

1324) We all have different paths to go upon in life but remember that no matter where our path takes us. We will always get through it.

1325) What should matter to us is not how other people see us but who we are deep down. So, let's focus on being true to ourselves today.

1326) When you believe in something, you are willing to fight for it so let's never give up on ourselves or anything worth believing in.

1327) Because of all lessons learned from making mistakes, I am living life with wisdom & clarity - that will never lead me astray again.

1328) Every morning when I wake up, I make a promise to myself that today will be the best of my life & every day I fulfill that promise.

1329) I cannot control what happens outside of myself but I can control how well I take care of my mind, body and spirit. So, let's do it.

1330) Nothing is ever as bad as it seems. So, let's stop over thinking, live in the moment and trust that everything happens for a reason.

1331) Taking control of our own happiness is the most important thing in life because when we're happy, everyone else feels the same way.

1332) There are only 2 things stopping me from achieving my goals: FEAR & Procrastination. So, I choose to overcome my fear & just do it.

1333) There is no need to go searching for happiness when it's going to find you anyways. You can trust me on this - it happens every day.

1334) Things keep getting better and better for me, which means that I'm being guided in the right direction. And that feels pretty great.

1335) Tonight I will dream great dreams where nothing goes wrong at all because tonight is just another way of saying "let go and trust."

1336) When times are tough don't give up because it will get better. Remember the sun rise everyday a new beginning for us to start over.

1337) Every positive thought attracts more positive thoughts into my mind, making my outlook on life only get better and better every day.

1338) I hope you know that today and every day after no matter what happens, I want you to remember something. I love you unconditionally.

1339) In order to gain happiness. you need to give it away first. So, smile and be kind because your kindness will always come back around.

1340) Our past only matters if we let it define who we are. So why don't we make that choice instead of letting others be in charge of it.

1341) The truth of the matter is, we won't always get along so let's move forward and learn how to deal with each other in a positive way.

1342) I will always keep smiling because I'm cute as a button. And speaking of buttons, push me once and I'll push you back twice harder.

1343) I've got an idea of what I want out of life but only my future can decide if I get it or not. So, let's make the best possible future.

1344) Life isn't perfect but if we give it time, we will grow and become better people through our mistakes and that's what really matters.

1345) Sometimes things get harder before they get easier which means let's challenge ourselves by doing something new every once in a while.

1346) We have been blessed with a lot in life. including another day to turn things around. So, let's live it up instead of wasting it away.

1347) When life throws us curveballs, we must learn from them and then move on to become better people because that's what true strength is.

1348) You can either worry about your past or you can create a future full of beautiful memories. So, let's take a step forward and do both.

1349) Always smile through the tears because no matter how much it hurts, there's always something beautiful to be found in every situation.

1350) I hope you know that today and every day after no matter what happens, I want you to remember something. I care about your wellbeing.

1351) If I don't like something then I change it. I'm not going to just sit back and wait for things to happen. let's go, we got work to do.

1352) I'm not perfect but at least I can admit it. And better still, now I know what needs improving & am actively doing something about it.

1353) Just let go of any worries you might have because they are irrational and not worth thinking about. Let's enjoy the present even more.

1354) Let's have a fun day but only if we put our minds to it because it is up to us how we spend our time. So, let's do what makes us happy.

1355) Let's not let anyone tell us who we should be or how we should act today because life isn't worth living if you aren't being yourself.

1356) No matter how much it hurts, or what obstacles stand in the way, each day holds an opportunity for me to succeed if I just keep going.

1357) Positivity brings about more positivity. That has always been the case, and it always will be. And right now, I choose to be positive.

1358) They might think they've got the world at their feet but they don't know that behind every successful man is a woman rolling her eyes.

1359) I don't have time for people who bring me down so their words do not mean anything. Let's keep the real ones close by and move forward.

1360) Our past does not define us - it simply shows us where we've been which means there is no need to stay stuck unless that's what we want.

1361) We are living in one of the best times ever to be alive which means it is essential for us all to make the most of every single moment.

1362) When we feel alone. let us remember that there is someone out there who cares and is willing to help without asking anything in return.

1363) "I have arrived" may not be an actual place but anywhere we want to go can become one because time is simply something our mind creates.

1364) Every day in life brings more and more happiness just waiting for me to experience it firsthand and why wouldn't I? Not me, not anybody.

1365) I'm grateful for my life and all of its great moments, big and small. And guess what? That makes every moment seem even more gratifying.

1366) It doesn't matter what anyone else says- ultimately the only person whose opinion matters is mine. So why not start believing in myself?

1367) Let's be kind to each other because no one knows the battles that others are facing which means they need our compassion more than ever.

1368) Let's remember that there is hope everywhere we look which means no matter how difficult everything gets, we will find peace eventually.

1369) The more positivity you have in your life, the easier everything becomes. And I'm having a lot of it right now so things are going well.

1370) Today I'm going to do something special for myself which means I should probably go and relax in the bathtub with some bubbles and wine.

1371) Today, tomorrow & every single day after that brings with it infinite possibilities - which means today can be whatever I want it to be.

1372) Turn on the happy switch because it makes everything go right when you do. and guess what? I turned it on. And now my day is going well.

1373) What happens in our lives are only tests that help us grow into better people, so let's just take them and see where we land in the end.

1374) When you get angry, think of all the things that made you angry throughout your entire life & then ask yourself: was it really worth it?

1375) Don't be afraid of your mind because even though it can hurt sometimes, there are always beautiful things being thought every single day.

1376) I will be brave enough to take risks in life because I am strong enough. I am smart enough. and I deserve all the good that comes my way.

1377) No matter what you go through always remember that there is a reason for everything and every situation. We all play a part in this life.

1378) Nobody else matters today except for me because I want to be at my best both physically and mentally so I can accomplish all of my goals.

1379) Some people will talk about me behind my back, that's the life I have so let's keep our projections up and not listen to their ignorance.

1380) Sometimes things aren't always as bad as they seem but instead of constantly worrying, use the time to appreciate the things you do have.

1381) We may not know who said these things but all that matters is how good they made us feel so why don't we make ourselves feel like queens?

1382) The more obstacles that appear before me only serve to make me stronger and every challenge is just another opportunity for me to shine.

1383) All my dreams are coming true with every positive affirmation that goes through my mind. Really, what could be better than that? Not much.

1384) Don't be afraid of challenges because they might just turn into something special. So, take the time to appreciate the small stuff in life.

1385) Every day has so many benefits packed into it no matter how difficult it may seem. That's just how life is and today will be no different.

1386) Every day is a new opportunity for us to make things right by setting higher standards with what we expect out of life. let's start today.

1387) I forgive myself for all the times I have not been loving to myself, forgiving them because they are in the past and no longer part of me.

1388) I have no room in my life for thoughts, beliefs or feelings that are not of unconditional love - so I now release them all with gratitude.

1389) I know how important it is for you to see your dreams realized so let's stay committed because we are close enough now it's time to dig in.

1390) The only limit that exists is the one that we put on ourselves so let's keep pushing forward no matter what other people try to do or say.

1391) All it takes for you to be happy is for you to believe that you are capable of being happy. So, let's do this today and every day hereafter.

1392) It's okay to feel tired sometimes but don't let anyone tell you how to feel because this is our life. we have to live it on our own accord.

1393) We may never know why these people act this way but does it really matter when there are more people out there without a reason to be kind?

1394) The most important principle for achieving success is knowing exactly what you want out of life and going after it with a burning passion.

1395) Every success leads to another success which allows me to continuously grow stronger, wiser, and more capable than before. I am unstoppable.

1396) I am one in 7 billion but that doesn't mean we can't all make an impact together because when we work together, we always make things happen.

1397) I can achieve anything I set my mind to so right now I will dream big and then I will take steps towards making those dreams become reality.

1398) I have to keep rising until everyone believes that I am unstoppable. that all it takes is a little push and I'll take over this whole world.

1399) If they really knew me. they wouldn't like me. So why do I bother caring about what people think when they'll never see what's in my heart?

1400) Past cannot be changed but the future can so let's not dwell on it and focus on what we want to become instead of trying to change the past.

1401) Sometimes you have to ignore people if they can't understand what matters most. us. So, let's be better than them and move forward. together.

1402) The truth of the matter is we aren't promised tomorrow so let's make the most of every single day because it can all be gone in a heartbeat.

1403) Today I'm setting out to make it a great day and nothing can stop me from doing that, not even me That's why today feels absolutely amazing.

1404) Two paths lie before me: one filled with shadows shrouded in fear & regret & the other lit up with self-love & passion for life. No contest.

1405) We all go through a lot in life but the truth of the matter is, you are going to come out on top as long as you work hard and never give up.

1406) If you're not pushing yourself then why are you even trying? Go all out right now if success is what you want because nothing else matters.

1407) Success is not a thing an individual can achieve, it is achieved by everyone. So why not give it a try? Everyone deserves to be successful.

1408) I am going to do my best today and also tomorrow because hard work doesn't go unnoticed which means I want all the praise that comes from it.

1409) Nothing good comes easy but if you really want something you've got to stop making excuses & go get it. So why don't we make this world ours.

1410) Positivity leads into greatness which leads into even more happiness than before. That sounds amazing, doesn't it? Well, that's because it is.

1411) We all have a story to tell which means let's write a new chapter about how we overcame adversities and became a better person because of it.

1412) When hard times come around, let's not forget that it will eventually get better. The sun rises every day, a new beginning for us to start over.

1413) I know that someone is always looking out for my best interests; therefore, I can trust that everything will be okay no matter what happens.

1414) I will not let my fears get in the way of accomplishing my dreams because I know if I keep pushing myself then nothing is impossible for me.

1415) Every time I think of something negative about myself or life, I will immediately shift my thoughts towards something positive and productive.

1416) Everyone gets knocked down in life, but it's how you get up that counts. So, let's get back on our feet before they can even touch the ground.

1417) Have faith in yourself and spread kindness everywhere because if everyone did that, there would be no fighting or wars. just peace everywhere.

1418) I know that we cannot control what others say or do but we can always control how we react to those things. So, let's be positive and thriving.

1419) I will continue to take steps towards achieving my dreams, no matter how small they might be. because every journey begins with a single step.

1420) I will never give someone else power over how I feel. this is my life and I'm taking control. So, if you don't like it then get out of my way.

1421) If you don't like something, change it. If you can't change it, accept it. And if you can't accept it, then change the way you think about it.

1422) Life is fantastic. But you know what would make it more fantastic than ever before? More success. Which means an easy street for me to follow.

1423) Positivity breeds positivity which brings about an even greater feeling of joy than before. And why wouldn't I want that? Not me, not anybody.

1424) Today there are so many benefits floating around me that I can't even begin to imagine what they all are. And that's exactly how it should be.

1425) I don't have time to worry about petty little things because my goals are right in front of me. I just have to stop worrying and start doing.

1426) If you want something, go for it. If you don't, move on and focus on worthy pursuits because life is too short not to do the things you love.

1427) It is possible for one human being to make another human being happy. Sometimes all it takes is a little effort. and sometimes no effort at all.

1428) Life is always giving me opportunities for growth, even when it doesn't seem like it. 1927) My thoughts are creating an abundant future for me.

1429) Sometimes people who are happy would rather look for something to complain about because it's easier than having to admit that they're blessed.

1430) We are all beautiful in our own way, so never doubt yourself again because I know the real you is way better than any fairytale story out there.

1431) Every day in life brings more happiness just waiting for me to experience it firsthand Can you believe that.? Well, believe it or not, it's true.

Year 5: Very long positive Affirmations for Pros

1432) Every day in life brings more success just waiting for me to experience it first-hand Can you believe that.? Well, believe it or not, it's true.

1433) I don't want anybody to interfere with my life so if you could just respect my decision then I would appreciate it. thank you for understanding.

1434) I look at the past as a learning experience so I don't want to get stuck there. I can do better than that so let's go out and prove it together.

1435) Let's be grateful for what we have instead of wanting more which means being happy with what you already have and use it to help others in need.

1436) Letting go. doesn't mean forgetting about someone it just means letting them go so they can find their true happiness which may not be with you.

1437) Life isn't always easy so when hard times come around. let's not forget that it will eventually get better. The sun always rises after the rain.

1438) Positivity breeds positivity which brings about an even greater sense of joy than before. So why would I go and ruin a good thing? Not this guy.

1439) Every day in life brings more and more happiness just waiting for me to experience it firsthand. I mean come on, what could be better than that?

1440) I know that my happiness and success lie within me and no one else has the power to take it away from me. So, let's make it clear where we stand.

1441) I will never allow anger or negativity to take root within me again because those emotions don't serve me and they certainly don't make me happy.

1442) If they only knew the real me. they wouldn't say half of the things they say. So, I'm going to do what I can, when I can, until they know my value.

1443) Let's start using this time as an opportunity to grow and appreciate that everyone makes mistakes, because that means they're human just like us.

1444) Love yourself for who you are and never forget that even if someone doesn't appreciate your worth. they weren't meant to be part of your journey.

1445) My thoughts are golden because positivity breeds more positivity. And why wouldn't I want that? So, here's to a great day full of golden thoughts.

1446) Today I am going to do what needs to be done because I know that failure isn't an option. I am prepared and ready to show everyone what I can do.

1447) We all want to live life in harmony which means let's love others and spread that positivity. People will eventually see the kind person you are.

1448) We do not have always measure up with society standards but that's because we have a vision that the world hasn't seen yet. So, let's keep going.

1449) You know why the sky is blue? Because it isn't green. So, let's start being different and change things up because that is what life is all about.

1450) Let's not waste time on negativity because that's all it will ever be - wasted time. So, let's change our lives instead of letting them control us.

1451) Overcoming adversity builds character so remember when your down. get back up and learn from your mistakes. Don't beat yourself up over past ones.

1452) When you're feeling down, remember that someone else has it way worse than you do so look at them and remember anything can be overcome with hope.

1453) Success comes to those who are patient enough to wait while others rush. If you can handle waiting, you will be rewarded with success in the end.

1454) Successful people do what unsuccessful people won't. I'm not going to let my fear stop me from taking the actions that I need to achieve success.

1455) The harder I push, the more successful I will be. My work ethic determines how far I go with my pursuits so there's no way that I'm slowing down.

1456) - When I wake up every morning, I am thankful because I know that living my dreams is possible. I just have to take the steps towards success first.

1457) I am not afraid of tomorrow because it will be another positive day in my life. I'm always looking for the silver lining and today is no different.

1458) I know how hard it is to stand alone in the middle of a storm so let's face our fear together and push through this like we always do. We got this.

1459) Life is precious and that's why we must treat everyone with respect because even if you don't know someone. they could still deserve your kindness.

1460) My dream comes true in every area of my life because I follow my heart's desires which always lead me towards happiness, joy, peace and fulfillment.

1461) Positivity leads into greatness which leads into even more positivity than before, day after day And I can't imagine why I'd want it any other way.

1462) The past can hurt but only if I allow it too. which means it's up to me if I want to let go and create my own future or stay stuck in old patterns.

1463) We all have dreams which means let's not give up on them because it will take time but I promise everything worthwhile will be worth it in the end.

1464) We are all strong when we are united so let's not allow anything to pull us apart today because no matter our differences, we're never truly alone.

1465) All I want to do today is be kind because the world needs more of that. I am so blessed for this opportunity so let's change up our energy together.

1466) Every time I have a good thought, it will work wonders for me today because positivity means success. And that's exactly what's happening right now.

1467) Everything is possible if we make it happen with our own hands. We are all in control of making the most out of life because everything is possible.

1468) My past does not dictate my future. Today is a new day and I'm going to make the best of it so please don't show up and expect me to be a pushover.

1469) Posit breeds positivity which brings about an even greater feeling of joy than before. And who would ever want anything different? Certainly not me.

1470) Sometimes we need time to reflect on our actions, recharge our batteries and dream about what could be. So why not take some breathing space today?

1471) The best people come into your life when you need them the most. So, let's treasure those unique relationships even though they may not last forever.

1472) We are all strong when we are united so let's not allow anything to pull you apart today because no matter our differences, we're never truly alone.

1473) We never know when life will be done with us so let's just treat everyone kindly and appreciate every minute that we have been given on this planet.

1474) We're all going to die and that's a fact but if we stop worrying about our life and start living it then we won't have any regrets in the end of it.

1475) I am the one who makes all the decisions in my life for better or worse, and if I ever need help, there's always somebody around to give me advice.

1476) I will give up all in life in order to gain success. If that means giving up my home and family, then so be it because success is what I want most.

1477) Every day is filled with all sorts of happiness, joy, and wonder thanks to the positive things in my life. Why would I want it any other way? Not me.

1478) Everyone gets knocked down sometimes but it's without a doubt in my mind that I WILL get back up with ease. I will appropriate this life for my own.

1479) I know how difficult it is to forgive yourself after you have made a mistake so if you don't mind, let's move on from the past and create our future.

1480) It's okay if they're not speaking to me now because one day, they'll see how much I've changed and they'll wish that they were still friends with me.

1481) It's okay to not be perfect because nobody is perfect on this earth which means just being ourselves is enough for others to love us unconditionally.

1482) Let's not forget to remind ourselves that we are always beautifully and wonderfully made. It doesn't matter what anyone says because we all got this.

1483) My past does not equal my future as long as I refuse to live in the shadows of my former self. So, let's start living for a brighter future right now.

1484) Remember that you don't have to be perfect because nobody is. we just have opportunities to learn from our mistakes and make ourselves better people.

1485) This world may try to bring us down with negativity but together we can spread love instead which means happiness is contagious so let's start today.

1486) When going through tough times, remember that other people are fighting battles too which means let's all look out for each other instead of against.

1487) You cannot start the next chapter of your life if you keep re-reading the last one; so, let's make today that day. Let's take control because we can.

1488) Can you hear me? I'm talking to you. As long as you're breathing then nothing is out of reach. So, close your eyes and imagine all the possibilities.

1489) I am enough. Just as I am right now. With all of my flaws, mistakes & whatever else you might think of me. - Which is why the world adores me so much.

1490) If something doesn't make sense anymore let's just say go on to something that's gone because there are things in life that are just not meant to be.

1491) Let's remember that there will never be another like us. ever. Which means embrace our uniqueness and use it towards making this world a better place.

1492) So let's just focus on making today great of worrying about tomorrow because life is happening now - and all we have to do is take full responsibility.

1493) You can either accept change or resist it which means try things out and be open to new things. Because change will always be around but so should we.

1494) I don't care how many times I fail because failure is only another way of saying "let's do this again but differently next time." It really is win/win.

1495) I know that sometimes, we all doubt ourselves but don't let anyone tell you how to feel because this is our life. we have to live it on our own accord.

1496) It might be complicated but it's worth fighting for. So, let's make today the day where we stand up for ourselves and take back what is rightfully ours.

1497) Let's see the bright side of life instead of focusing on the negative because no matter how bad it seems, there's always a positive to every situation.

1498) My attitude determines how well everything goes today because positivity attracts positive things into my life. I'm fully prepared for a wonderful day.

1499) No matter how far away he is or how long it takes him to come back. I will always wait for him. Because I believe in true love and that will never end.

1500) One of the best ways to show our worth is by being ourselves. Let's make it a mission and help others do the same.

1501) The world needs more people like us who are willing to banish negative thoughts into oblivion without begging for forgiveness. Let's make a difference.

1502) Today is another chance to start over so let's not waste it by doing the same things that lead us here again. live life to the fullest potential today.

1503) Every day is a brand-new beginning full of endless possibilities with infinite opportunities to manifest my dreams and goals easily and effortlessly now.

1504) I am going to take every opportunity that comes my way and I will never give up on my dreams because we were given this life to live it to the fullest.

1505) Let's stop worrying about what other people want us to do because remember: we only live one life so let's make it memorable by doing something we love.

1506) We may not know these people but that doesn't mean their negativity has to affect us. So, let's be better than them instead of letting them bring us down.

1507) When you feel good about where you're at in life, the only place left for you to go is up Which means success is waiting for me right around the corner.

1508) You can do anything if you put your mind to it. Never doubt yourself again because I know the real you is way better than any fairytale story out there.

1509) If it wasn't meant for anyone to accomplish their dreams then why would they be there? There's always a path towards success, you just have to find it.

1510) Every day in life brings more and more happiness just waiting for me to experience it firsthand. Can you believe that.? Well, believe it or not, it's true.

1511) I believe in myself. I think positively. I work hard. and I always go after what I want which means everything is possible because I will make it happen.

1512) I will not let my problems define me, instead I will let my actions define me and then stand tall & smile knowing that everything works out for the best.

1513) If we think positive then our attitude will reflect that which sends good vibes out into the universe asking for wonderful things to come into our lives.

1514) It doesn't matter how many times we fall down. it is about getting back up and continuing with our journey which means learning from our mistakes is key.

1515) Positivity breeds positivity which brings about an even greater feeling of joy than before. And who would ever want anything different? Certainly not me.

1516) Remember that the past is behind you but the future is bright ahead. So, let's put on some sunglasses and just enjoy our journey in life. time is ticking.

1517) Sometimes what breaks us is the very thing that helps us grow so remember when life gives you lemons, use them to heal yourself when you're feeling down.

1518) All of the knowledge and all of the wealth in this world is useless without a smile to share it with. So, let's keep going until we have all that and more.

1519) Every day in life brings more and more happiness just waiting for me to experience it firsthand. Can you believe that.? Well, believe it or not, it's true.

1520) A positive attitude is the key to success. When you lose hope, remember that everything will work out in time and trust yourself- even when times seem dark or difficult.

1521) Let's remember mistakes are best opportunities for growth which means if something bad happens to us, learn from it and make sure it doesn't happen again.

1522) People may try to keep me down but it's not going to work because I am determined and passionate and that is a rare combination. So, they better watch out.

1523) Positivity breeds positivity which brings about an even greater sense of joy than before. And what could possibly be wrong with that? Not me, not anybody.

1524) No matter what happens today I'm going to keep pushing forward because tomorrow will bring new opportunities for greatness. I don't stop so why should I?

1525) I welcome all opportunities with open arms, no matter how big or small they may be because you never know when your dreams are going to knock at your door.

1526) I will always have something to look forward to- even when it doesn't seem like that right now. So let go of the bad and trust that the good is on its way.

1527) Moving on is never the best option but letting go is so let's just get rid of all that baggage you're carrying around and move on with our lives. shall we?

1528) People are so caught up in their own lives that they don't even realize how much better life could be if they just took the time to stop & smell the roses.

1529) Questioning lets us explore different paths and ideas which means let's ask questions instead of judging people based off their appearance or how they act.

1530) The only thing stopping me from having the best day of my life today is me, because I'm already doing everything right That feels pretty great, doesn't it?

1531) We all have good times and bad but learn from both. Let go of your past because you're never going to find anything if you keep looking in the same places.

1532) When we look up at the stars in the night sky, we hear a little voice inside us that says we can do anything we set our minds to. what does your voice say?

1533) Every time things do not work out as planned, no matter how difficult it may seem, there is always something positive that can be taken from the situation.

1534) Expecting great things to happen makes them become reality because that's how powerful my thoughts are when I think positively. That's the way it should be.

1535) People shouldn't judge a book by its cover because everyone has a story which means before making assumptions about someone, try getting to know them first.

1536) Sometimes it feels like everything around us is falling apart but remember, if you keep pushing forward. you'll find those beautiful rays of sunshine again.

1537) When my feet hit the floor each morning, I make a promise to myself that today will be the best day ever. and guess what? So far, every single day has been.

1538) If you want success, then prove yourself first. Show them what you can do before asking for a handout or a promotion. Work hard first, ask questions later.

1539) I am lovable and loveable - regardless of any past or future mistakes, regardless of any past or future problems, regardless of any past or future successes.

1540) It's time to start this day over because it doesn't come with a manual. So, let's make today a different one. one in which we don't repeat the same mistakes.

1541) I've spent too many years being sad about things I can't control so why not focus on the things I can??? Like myself for example. I am totally controllable.

1542) Keeping an attitude of gratitude brings about beautiful moments into my life on a daily basis. That sounds pretty wonderful, right? Well, that's because it is.

1543) Never give up on yourself or your dreams because there's no such thing as a little pregnant. if you want something, go for it and don't take no as an answer.

1544) Positivity breeds more positivity so if I feel good right now, think positively about the future, and take action, everything will be better than ever before.

1545) Sometimes I feel like giving up on myself but then I realize that no one else can tell me what to do. So, let's start this new year off with some self-belief.

1546) The first step to making anything happen is deciding that it will happen, then the next step is putting in the time and effort required to make it come true.

1547) We all have problems so let's not judge others because we don't know the best way out is through so stay positive and keep pushing no matter how hard it gets.

1548) - My life's purpose is to live a life full of happiness and success. All aspects of my life are heading towards this purpose so I have nothing to worry about.

1549) Life isn't always easy so when hard times come around. let's not forget that it will eventually get better. It may seem dark but just look. the sun is rising.

1550) Positivity breeds positivity which leads into greatness just like a house built upon a rock: firm and unshakable So why would I want it any other way? Not me.

1551) The moment you stop believing in yourself is the moment where opportunity stops knocking on your door so let's be thankful for what we have and keep dreaming.

1552) We need to worry less about what other people think and more about being the best versions of ourselves which means we should be our own biggest cheerleaders.

1553) Be grateful for all of the stress in your life because it's helping you learn and grow as a person. You can't know where your potential is until you test it.

1554) If you can't make a choice, remember you'll take more from life by not choosing than if you choose wrong so don't be afraid to stay still every once in a while.

1555) Let's love ourselves for who we are because nobody is perfect which means knowing your flaws like the back of your hand and still loving yourself despite them.

1556) Let's stop worrying about what people think and focus on our own happiness because you can't make everyone happy all the time. So, make sure YOU'RE happy today.

1557) My latest mistake was only a lesson waiting to happen. So, let's all stop beating around the bush and instead just get straight into learning from our mistakes.

1558) Nothing gets past me today because positivity breeds more positivity which leads to greatness. So why wouldn't I do that every single day? It just makes sense.

1559) We all have problems so let's not judge others because we don't know. the best way out is through so stay positive and keep pushing no matter how hard it gets.

1560) A wise man knows when to hold back and when to go after his dreams. I'm seizing this day like my dream is on fire and there's no room for hesitation or doubt.

1561) No one decides your happiness but you. So, stop making decisions based on what other people think or say because eventually their thoughts are going to change.

1562) We all have problems in life but what matters most is knowing how to overcome them which means use your knowledge and wisdom towards becoming a stronger person.

1563) If you are going through a tough time right now then I want you to know that whatever it is, it will only make us stronger when we choose to fight for our lives.

1564) I'm only one person but together, we can make the world a better place. There are people in need and I can help them by doing even just one small thing each day.

1565) Let's learn how to end each day with grace because tomorrow has no guarantees which means let's end today on a positive note and enjoy the little things in life.

1566) We all make mistakes and feel like we aren't good enough but this isn't true. we are born perfect and life's challenges make us stronger plus we learn from them.

1567) It's time for me to stop thinking about what other people think of me and start believing in who I am because the only one holding me back from greatness is me.

1568) A lot of people think that changing themselves is the only way to be accepted by someone else when in reality they should just accept themselves for who they are.

1569) Even though that person hurt me, why should I worry about them anymore? It doesn't matter because I'm focusing on bettering myself and making my dreams come true.

1570) Forgive yourself for making mistakes. What's done is done but it doesn't mean that we have to forget about them or let them hold us back. let go and move forward.

1571) I know I am not perfect but I can always give 110% because nobody else will do that for me. I am committed to doing better every single day and you should be too.

1572) I know if I am unhappy with my life, it's because of the choices I've made to create that reality - so today is a new day & as of this moment, I choose happiness.

1573) I love myself unconditionally, just as I am. - And because I love myself unconditionally, there are infinite possibilities for me to explore in life. So, let's go.

1574) If you keep treating me this way then I have no choice but to release you from my life because your happiness means more to me than my own. I hope you understand.

1575) My own attitude determines whether things go well or not - which means when I feel like giving up, I need to look inside myself because that's where my power lies.

1576) I choose to believe that everything is happening for a reason because it could be the small piece of knowledge, we need to evolve into better versions of ourselves.

1577) I don't care what people think of me because at the end of the day all that matters is that I am happy with myself. So, let's work together to get rid of self-harm.

1578) I'm alive today. which means no matter how bad it seems or feels there's always something for me to be happy about. So, let's find that thing & make this day great.

1579) It's okay not to be okay but even better when you can turn it around with a smile on your face. 820) Remember that you don't have to be perfect. because nobody is.

1580) Our time here on earth is short but our impact can last for eternity so let's help each other out as much as we possibly can before we all leave this world behind.

1581) We all make mistakes even if it was an accident because nobody is perfect which means the next time we do, just forgive yourself and never make the same one again.

1582) The only limits that exist within our lives are ones we place upon ourselves. No one can tell me that a certain goal is too far out of reach for me to accomplish.

1583) When you feel like quitting, think of how good it'll feel when you're done doing what you hated doing. You can make it through anything if you give yourself hope.

1584) I am not going to listen to anyone who doesn't believe in me because if they aren't helping, then they are holding me back. So, let's ignore everyone and just do us.

1585) It's important to take steps towards your dreams but don't forget to stop and appreciate everything you have in front of you. a wonderful future is waiting for you.

1586) Life is unpredictable but you know what? That's okay because uncertainty means "I haven't made up my mind yet" which means I am free to make whatever choice I want.

1587) Remember no matter how bad things get, they can only get better if we give them that chance. So, let's just work it out together because love always wins in the end.

1588) Sometimes it's easy to forget that everyone makes mistakes because we don't see the whole picture. So, remember, everyone is fighting battles you know nothing about.

1589) Self-doubt is only there to make you stronger on your path towards greatness. You are capable of more than what others think, so show them all how capable you are.

1590) Everything happens for a reason even if sometimes I don't understand why. but life can change in an instant so anything could be just around the corner (good or bad)

1591) I'm alive today and that means no matter how bad it seems or feels there's always something for me to be happy about. So, let's find that thing & make this day great.

1592) Let's not get distracted by the little things people say and do which means ignoring what they think or even how they treat us, because we can't control them anyway.

1593) No matter how stressed or overwhelmed I may feel at times, everything always works out for me. I just have to trust that this moment will unfold the way it needs to.

1594) Sometimes it feels like I could be doing so much better than what I currently am but then it dawns on me that as long as my best is always improving, then so will I.

1595) The secret ingredient to living an extraordinary life is giving up on being perfect. because nothing is ever "perfect" anyway so why waste time trying to make it so?

1596) Stop thinking of the obstacles in your way and start using them as motivation to succeed. The more difficult something is the greater the reward once it's achieved.

1597) I am not afraid of anything except being too scared to live. I choose every day to move forward with courage instead of letting fear hold me back. that is my victory.

1598) I live a great life now because of all the good things that have happened. And it makes me believe even more in positive thinking So why not think positively, right?

1599) If we all take care of each other instead of worrying about ourselves, the world would be such a wonderful place so remember to help anyone you can when they need it.

1600) We're all different but that just means we get the chance to experience new things and understand each other which means let's use our differences and stand together.

1601) I'm not afraid or worried about anything because everything that could go wrong has already happened, and I still made it through unscathed. Now is my time to shine.

1602) Fear is just anticipation with a different name. It's common for people to be scared of the unknown but it only takes one step at a time. So, let's make today that day.

1603) Remember we can't always be strong. So, let's tell our friends when we need help instead of pretending we don't, because it's okay to ask for assistance when you need it.

1604) You shouldn't judge people for their past because it's what they've been through that made them who they are today. So, let's celebrate the differences before we judge.

1605) I choose to believe in my ability to succeed because that's what I do best. I can't afford to doubt myself or give up on my dreams because it will all be for nothing.

1606) I will become more successful than ever before so long as I never give up on myself. Nothing is impossible, not when it comes to achieving greatness within our lives.

1607) I will stand atop the world because I've worked harder than anyone else out there. It doesn't matter if everyone thinks I'm crazy it only matters that I'm successful.

1608) When times are tough, remember; it's not how you fall that matters, but rather how you get back up again. It's all about picking yourself up and dusting yourself off.

1609) You're never going to live up to your full potential unless you push yourself harder than ever before. If greatness is what you want then get out there and pursue it.

1610) Everything happens for a reason, no matter what that reason is. let's believe that it's going to be okay. Remember today is a new beginning, a fresh start just for you.

1611) If you like something, let everyone know. Don't be afraid of rejection and hesitation because if we don't express our feelings how will we know if we feel the same way?

1612) If you want to see what's going on in my head then look behind me because I'm walking away. So please stop playing games and accept that if the shoe fits. then wear it.

1613) It's easy to get caught up in what everyone else is saying but today let's just focus on the positive things for the people who want nothing more than for us to succeed.

1614) Let's stop caring about what other people think because it leads to an unfulfilled life and never knowing what we truly want because we're too busy listening to others.

1615) My mind has been renewed with positivity and now I see the world through that lens. Who wouldn't want to see the world through that type of thinking.? Not me, for sure.

1616) There are a lot of people out there who want to turn their back on me but I am not going to give them the satisfaction because I know what they don't. I'm going places.

1617) There's always hope and there's always more chances to come which means never forget that no matter how bad things get, you can slowly recover from it so hang in there.

1618) Wow. Look at all the great things happening in my life right now. It's like this is the best time in the history of everything -not that there could ever be a bad time.

1619) If I don't live my life to the fullest, then what do I have to look forward to? Stagnation is death so why not keep pushing forward until I'm successful beyond belief.

1620) The only way you're going to make any progress is by pushing yourself harder than anyone else. You want success? Then show everyone how bad you want it, day after day.

1621) Every day presents an opportunity for betterment which means every day promises positivity if we make sure to look for it instead of finding excuses why it won't happen.

1622) It's okay to not have all the answers, just remember there are others who do. And if no one has it. you can find it yourself by doing research or learning more about it.

1623) Let's look ahead towards our future with bright eyes and a smile because it will take us exactly where we want to be. So, let's work as hard as we can and make it happen.

1624) The most beautiful thing in life is that we're all different and unique which means never forgetting to be yourself because it's the only thing you can truly call yours.

1625) We may never know who these people are but does it really matter anyway? Maybe they're happier than us. So, let's be positive instead of wondering about their negativity.

1626) Sometimes people play games when they're scared of getting hurt themselves. So just remember that even though you don't mean anything to them. you mean everything to you.

1627) The best way to get something you want is by saving up for it instead of constantly spending your hard-earned money on useless items that break easily or don't last long.

1628) Every day there are plenty of reasons for me to feel good and today happens to be one of those days. And why wouldn't it? Not with all the positivity floating around here.

1629) I can make a difference in this world by positively impacting other people's lives which means I need to live every day as if it was my last because life is too important.

1630) I've learned from past successes and failures and now I'm able to apply all lessons learned so that I can continue growing & moving forward no matter what life throws my way.

1631) Let's not look back. because it wastes time, energy and space in our heads that can be used for more positive things instead. Let's constantly learn from them and move on.

1632) Remember that no matter what. we all have the capability of making the world a better place just by loving each other. Let's take that chance to change the world together.

1633) Every obstacle presents an opportunity to succeed, you just need the right mindset to utilize it. Let go of your fears and push forward if you want something out of life.

1634) Life rewards those who take risks and persevere over those who doubt themselves and dream big without putting in the effort to achieve those dreams. So why not start now?

1635) A new level of positivity is here right now and I'm setting out to embrace it just like a long-lost friend That feels pretty amazing, doesn't it? Well, that's because it is.

1636) At the end of the day, life is too short for me to spend my time on people who won't even try to understand me. So why don't I choose to surround myself with people who do?

1637) Getting up early creates a positive mood and helps us finish things that need to be done before the end of the day like studying for exams or cleaning our rooms before bed.

1638) Sometimes people don't notice what's staring them in the face. that you are a person with feelings who deserves to be treated with respect so please do better from now on.

1639) Stop trying to hold on to something that doesn't want to be held on to.) It may seem like a challenge at first but trust me it is way easier than what you're already doing.

1640) Today is a new day, with new opportunities and experiences which means we don't need to worry about the past. It's done, it's over and today is what I choose to make of it.

1641) The world around us is full of people who settled towards their goals. I'm not going to fall into that trap, I'm going to keep pushing forward until greatness is achieved.

1642) It doesn't matter if I'm a bit quiet today or not - sometimes we need a day to relax, be quiet & recharge the batteries which means there isn't a single thing to worry about.

1643) Let's stop stressing over things that aren't even worth our tear ducts because it's all going to pass anyway. Nothing last forever so live for today and let go of yesterday.

1644) There are times where we don't feel like moving but we need to remember that what doesn't kill us only makes us stronger. So, let's use those words as fuel and go after them.

1645) We need to realize now that we are so much more than what society says we should want or be which means feeling satisfied with ourselves is the first step towards happiness.

1646) Imagine what others would say if they heard about all of your failures? How far do you think they would come down on you? Play roulette with your life and see what happens.

1647) The world around us might not always make sense but do yourself a favor and keep pushing forward anyway. It doesn't matter how hard things get, only that you never give up.

1648) I possess the power to achieve anything if I just believe that for a second. which means we need to get out of our comfort zones sometimes in order to grow and become better.

1649) I'm not here by accident - there's a reason why I was born exactly when I was & where I am. all of this happened so that today could unfold the way it is unfolding right now.

1650) It doesn't matter what happened yesterday or how long it takes. we can achieve our dreams if we never give up on them. Let's start right now by taking positive steps forward.

1651) It's okay if this doesn't go according to plan because something better is waiting for us around the corner. Trust me on this one, it will all work out in the end. I promise.

1652) The world will judge me based on my actions but there is nothing anyone can say about me unless I allow them too. So, let's make sure we always protect ourselves with silence.

1653) While life can be unpredictable. it can also surprise you when you least expect it but why wait? We should be chasing down our dreams so today let's start making them happen.

1654) If you want to become truly successful then you have to let go of your fears, turn off the negative thoughts in your head, and start believing that it's possible for anyone.

1655) This isn't my moment, this is our moment. We all get the same amount of time in life so why waste any second doubting what you can achieve? You can do it too if you believe.

1656) People spend too much time with negativity and drama and that truly affects their happiness. we only have one life so why not live it in a positive way? Let's do it together.

1657) We are all special but there is nobody else like me. you are your own person so don't ever think you are stuck being someone else. this is your time to shine so let's do this.

1658) When life knocks me down, that's when my true character reveals itself. Will I get up and try again or will I let this defeat define who I am? This moment decides everything.

1659) When the sun sets today, I'm not going to think about how hard everything was, instead I'll think about how far I've come and how much closer I am towards achieving greatness.

1660) If at first you don't succeed, dust yourself off and try again. you'll get there eventually. The time will pass even if things seem hard now because the sun is rising up ahead.

1661) The only thing that stands between myself and happiness is ME. ME. ME. As soon as I figure out how to take care of me then I can have everything that's waiting for me to pick it up.

1662) There isn't anything stopping all the greatness from happening today because today is going to be yet another fantastic addition to this story, we call life. And who'd want that.

1663) When you're having a bad day, just remember that someone somewhere has been dealt way worse than you and yet they're still smiling. That should definitely count for something.

1664) Write down your feelings because it helps make them feel more real, which means you're not alone in how you're feeling and we should never be afraid to write down our thoughts.

1665) I will get everything I set out to achieve today because I've got more success stored up inside of me than even I know about. The only way I'm stopping is if I quit on myself.

1666) Don't ever think you're not talented or pretty enough because we all have unique qualities that make us special. Remember that next time someone says something unkind about you.

1667) I give myself permission to follow my heart because I know that I am going the right way when the path is unclear. Let's trust ourselves enough to take control of our own lives.

1668) I know it's difficult to love yourself but I want you to know that I am proud of you because after all, loving someone else is nothing without the ability to love yourself first.

1669) The only way to achieve true happiness is by being good-natured despite what happens around us because remember, bad things happen but there are always opportunities for growth.

1670) We all have problems so let's not judge others because we don't know what a person is going through and if we can, let's try our best to help even just one person in need today.

1671) Animals are living things too and we shouldn't hurt them for no reason which means caring for everything on this planet equally is important as it makes the world a better place.

1672) I am enough just as I was made: exactly how I'm supposed to be today So why not give myself a break and learn how much better things are when you're happy with yourself instead?

1673) I am filled with positivity right now and today just happens to be the best day of my life. Is it possible for anything better than this.? Yes, it is. So, keep thinking positively

1674) You can never stop thinking about someone or something once they have touched your heart. Let's allow ourselves to be loved unconditionally by someone special. We all deserve it.

1675) A new level of positivity is here right now and I'm setting out to embrace it with every ounce of energy that I have. And why wouldn't I? That sounds pretty fantastic, doesn't it.?

1676) I am going to set goals for myself because it's better to have something to work towards instead of always living with regret. Let's achieve greatness together through positivity.

1677) Positivity breeds positivity which leads into greatness just like a house built upon a rock: firm and unshakable. So why wouldn't I want that every day? It sounds pretty darn good.

1678) Positivity breeds positivity which leads into greatness which means the sky is the limit when it comes to how good I can feel.

1679) The future belongs to those who believe in their dreams. So today I am going to dream big and then achieve whatever it is that I want because where there is a will there is a way.

1680) The sky is never going to fall down- only my perspective of the can do that. So, let's work on changing my perspective, rebuilding myself & continuing to fly high like a good bird.

1681) Why do I always attract the same type of person? Because it's my shadow side that draws them to me, so by focusing on developing it - I draw in different types of people into my life.

1682) No matter how many times life knocks me down, I know that tomorrow will be better today. All of my past failures have led me to where I am today so I will continue standing tall.

1683) Don't worry about what other people think of you because it will never bring you down. because one day you will realize that all of your hard work has paid off. So, let's celebrate.

1684) Presence of mind leads to presence in life. So why not take a moment to breathe, live in the now and enjoy each breath I take because it takes me one step closer towards my dreams.

1685) The more I want things to change, the more they stay the same; because if I'm not willing to do anything different then why should anything change? (So, what will I do differently?)

1686) Everyone is different but that doesn't mean your life isn't meaningful because remember, your path is different than someone else's so don't waste time comparing yourself to others.

1687) I get to experience all the best things in life because of who I am and how far I've come, not just because of something outside myself. And isn't that incredible.? Of course, it is.

1688) My Life is overflowing with abundance and there isn't much I won't be able to accomplish if I put my mind to it. So why wouldn't I push myself as hard as possible? Because I can, that's why.

1689) Let's not compare ourselves to others and focus more on ourselves and the journey we're going through right now which means happiness comes from within not from everyone around you.

1690) I get to experience all the best things in life because of who I am and how far I've come, not just something outside myself. And isn't that incredible.? Of course it is.

1691) I will accomplish my dreams because I have faith in myself, faith that I can overcome anything put up against me. Life doesn't need to be easy as long as I never give up on myself.

1692) Success comes from helping others which means you should never look for a shortcut because they will always lead to failure. Just keep going straight and you'll get there eventually.

1693) There isn't anything stopping all the greatness from happening today because today is going to be yet another fantastic addition to this story, we call life. And who doesn't want that.

1694) I'm going to stop thinking about what could go wrong and start believing in what I can do. Don't regret the chances you missed, focus on all of the chances that are coming your way.

1695) All my dreams are coming true one at a time which means today will be another fantastic addition to the story of me. That sounds pretty amazing, doesn't it? Well, that's because it is.

1696) I can do anything I set my mind to because all of the excuses are gone now. It is only me, myself, and I. And I know that with a little bit of hard work I can accomplish great things.

1697) Let's make mistakes once in a while because it makes us human. which means caring too much about what other people think of us is pointless when all they do is make judgements anyway.

1698) When life gets hard. remember to take deep breaths and keep pushing through because everyone feels like giving up sometimes but it's how we overcome those struggles that help us grow.

1699) Mistakes are only made when someone refuses to learn from them. Your past doesn't have to dictate your future so why not fight today so tomorrow can be everything you've ever wanted?

1700) If you want to be rich then stop focusing on the money and start focusing on what you can do with it because there is more to life than just bills. Just go out there and seize the day.

1701) I'm sorry for whatever has happened to you but today, let's smile because life isn't about having a perfect past. it's about being able to move on and look forward for better tomorrow.

1702) Money is just a tool that facilitates living an amazing life - whether I have money or not it won't matter because I'm doing what makes me happy which means that every day will be great.

1703) There are times where I would almost sell my soul for another chance to do it right but at the end of the day, I know that this is all part of my journey. So, let's keep pushing forward.

1704) There isn't anything stopping all the greatness from happening today because today is going to be yet another fantastic addition to this story, we call life. And who wouldn't want that.

1705) We always think our whole world has fallen apart when actually all that happens is that life changes directions - which means there isn't a single thing for us to be stressed out about.

1706) A whole new level of positivity is here right now and I'm setting out to embrace it with every ounce of energy that I have.

1707) No one is going to hand me life on a silver platter and if I want it then I'm going to have to give my soul away. So, let's keep it real. I'm not willing to kill for anything anymore.

1708) Sometimes people are just destined to be in our lives for a reason, no matter how long or short it may be. We will never know what the future holds All we can do is live in the moment.

1709) We all should be kind to those around us no matter what they do or how they look because no one is perfect and there is always someone who loves them even if they don't love themselves.

1710) We might have been kicked down multiple times before but it wasn't for nothing because it made us stronger as individuals. So, let's keep going and don't let the negativity get you down.

1711) I am always one step ahead of whatever challenges may come from today. There is nothing that can stop me from succeeding because my goal is to be successful and it is written in stone.

1712) I choose success because I know failure is not an option for me anymore. It doesn't matter how many times I fall, because every time I get back up, I know my abilities increase tenfold.

1713) When you experience hard times, understand that these are necessary evils. Just because something is evil does not mean it is necessarily bad. It all depends on how you look at things.

1714) Let's not worry about what other people think and focus on how we feel and who we want to become because you're your own person and life is too short to waste it trying to please others.

1715) Life is overflowing with abundance and there isn't much I won't be able to accomplish if I put my mind to it.

1716) We all make mistakes in life but what matters most is how we recover from those mistakes. Don't allow yourself to fall apart during tough times, remain calm and focus on moving forward.

1717) I'm okay with where I am because at least it's a starting point - so let's all stop underestimating our potential and get started living our dreams already because we owe it to ourselves.

1718) Life is overflowing with abundance and there isn't much I won't be able to accomplish if I put my mind to it.

1719) Life is too short to be anything but happy and I'm not going to waste another minute. I am determined to live through this storm because the sunshine on the other side is calling my name.

1720) Life isn't always easy but overcoming challenges only makes us stronger and wiser. The sun will keep on rising with every day that passes by, time will heal everything. Just wait and see.

1721) There isn't much in life that would ever get me down because there are so many positive things happening every day to keep me going. Which means success is always right around the corner.

1722) We should always take pride in our actions because what we do says a lot about who we are. If you want people to respect you then you need to start respecting yourself first and foremost.

1723) My life is beautiful and wonderful, I am grateful for all the wonderful things that are happening to me.

1724) If you are not failing then you are not really trying so let's challenge ourselves every single day of our lives. Success will come knocking at our door if we can be patient enough.

1725) It doesn't matter whether or not we make mistakes as long as we learn from them. Life is full of surprises so stay on your toes and hold onto what really matters because nothing else does.

1726) We want success but success doesn't come without failure so it's okay if we fail because we will learn from our mistakes and strive for victory next time around. Just keep pushing forward.

1727) If I give up today, then what hope do I have of success tomorrow? Success comes to those who are willing to work for it so if I stop pushing forward, then my dreams are dead in the water.

1728) Remember to be kind and help others in need because you never know if one day the favor will be returned. Always smile, even when it hurts because something good is bound to come out of it.

1729) Today I am going to believe in my ability to be great because I know that nobody can stop me from being awesome. Let's work together since we have so many things to do now. life is calling.

1730) Every day is a good one because every day I have so many things to be thankful for. That includes thinking positively about what I want out of life. And following through makes it come true.

1731) My past does not determine my future- only the decisions I make today will shape it. So let go of any negative energy that wants to hold me back & trust that everything happens for a reason.

1732) Positivity breeds positivity which leads into greatness just like a house built upon a rock. Success is just about the only thing I want out of life. And I'm already getting it.

1733) I am my most successful when everything around me is falling apart and everyone thinks that I'm failing. This doesn't slow me down though because failure sounds like a challenge to my ears.

1734) People will say no. They will refuse us. And they could try to bring us down but we can't allow any of this negativity to affect our dreams which means staying strong and having faith is key.

1735) There is this odd fear deep down inside myself that one day, I am either going to lose everything or not be able to turn back the clock. So, let's live in the moment and enjoy it while we can.

1736) You are one in 7 billion, that's how rare you are so even if your journey is different than someone else's, you shouldn't feel discouraged because it makes you even more special to the world.

1737) I am going to push myself harder than ever before and make this year my best yet. There's nothing stopping me from achieving all of my dreams today except for doubt in myself. That ends now.

1738) Everyone makes mistakes but what really matters is knowing how to fix those mistakes which means every time life gives you lemons make lemonade with them instead of feeling sorry for yourself.

1739) Everything is going right for me because I know dwelling on the past only makes things worse. Why would I dwell when there is so much goodness waiting ahead of me?

1740) Success keeps knocking on my door, over and over again. And today just happens to be the day where I answer and let it in.

1741) Where there is darkness let's bring light instead of trying to save people who don't want to change which means we need to love ourselves too much to waste time on things that aren't worth it.

1742) If you're lucky enough to be different then don't forget who you truly are when all the world tries to curl you into their mold. You were made out of greatness so shine bright like a diamond.

1743) Let go of your fears and take control over your thoughts so you can focus on doing the things that matter most. You will succeed as long as you don't give up and keep fighting no matter what.

1744) The future belongs to those who take chances so instead of waiting around for good luck or for life to give me opportunities, I'm going to create them myself through hard work and dedication.

1745) Every day in life brings more happiness than ever before. And won't you want some of that too? Of course you do. So, start getting into positive thinking today - even if it's just for 5 minutes.

1746) If you want something bad enough, never give up until you've achieved your dreams because they will be worth more than anything in the world when we do. So let's keep pushing forward every day.

1747) It breaks my heart sometimes knowing how much pain you are going through even though you do your best not to show it because what doesn't kill us only makes us stronger. So, let's keep fighting.

1748) There are times when I feel like giving up but then I remember that quitting would mean that all of my hard work was for nothing. I'm going to push forward until there's no more "forward" left.

1749) You are probably thinking why is she telling me about her struggles but the truth of the matter is that we all go through things at different times. So, let's be understanding, that's all I ask.

1750) If you want a better future then you have to stop letting your past define you. Let go of your doubts and start believing that there's a bright tomorrow waiting just around the corner for you.

1751) To succeed, one must simply lead from their heart and not from their mind. If you want something bad enough, you will do whatever it takes to make it a reality. No ifs, ands, or buts about it.

1752) I will always keep fighting for truth, justice and the right way. They might be laughing now but just remember that when you're successful they'll be the ones saying "I knew them when...".

1753) Let's be grateful for this day because we never know what tomorrow holds. Remember to smile, laugh and enjoy life even on the bad days because things could always turn around for us any day now.

1754) The thing about being yourself is that no matter what, someone will always have a problem with it. but the only way you'll never regret anything in life is by staying true to who you really are.

1755) The time that we waste dwelling on other people's mistakes or hatred could instead be used recreating something better for ourselves which means changing others doesn't mean changing themselves.

1756) Everything is perfect. From this point forward, I'm allowing things to be easy for me. There are no challenges that I need to face, because everything is unfolding perfectly in my life right now.

1757) Money comes to money people; not to those who are moping around feeling sorry for themselves. So, stop feeling sorry for yourself and get busy doing whatever it takes for you to make more money today.

1758) Only change if your heart says yes and not by what people say which means don't be afraid of taking risk or trying new things because that's how we learn and who knows you might actually enjoy it.

1759) Sometimes we need to leave people behind even though they are meant to stay in our lives forever. but it doesn't mean that we stop caring. So, let's show them how much they mean through our actions.

1760) The world is full of negativity so if you see something wrong, spend some time making it right because we only get one chance at this thing called life. and it starts today so let's make it count.

1761) Don't waste time thinking about where you could be because you are already exactly where you need to be. The only way to make the best out of your current situation is by focusing on what's next.

1762) Don't think so much and just go with the flow because life is way too short for us to constantly question things. Just let reality unfold and take it one step at a time so we don't get overwhelmed.

1763) I wish everyone was just like me which means I need to be better than me if I want them to change their ways. Let's not be fake. it isn't worth it because eventually everyone will see through that.

1764) It's time for all the good stuff to happen and I'm ready for it because positive thinking has opened up these pathways of success like never before. And who would want to close them again.? Not me.

1765) Sometimes we need somebody fighting our battles for us because it's just too much but don't worry, even though they are on your side, you will still get stronger. So, let's get through this together.

1766) Success isn't achieved through magic, it's earned through self-discipline. Stop looking for shortcuts and start doing the work today if you don't want tomorrow to pass without making any progress.

1767) Do not be discouraged when it seems like nothing is happening in your life. Every day, success finds its way to me and if you choose the right perspective then this will happen for you too. Start getting into positive thinking today- even if just for five minutes of so can make all the difference with how we feel throughout each succeeding hour.

1768) It's not their life so why should they be involved? If they don't like us then let's just let it go. because people who do nothing but try to bring us down are only showing their own insecurities.

1769) My soul overflows with happiness and contentment and that means that nothing can bring me down because my eyes are focused on the positive side of things. And why wouldn't they be, I mean it's great.

1770) Get rid of your habit of waiting for things to happen because you'll be sitting around a long time wondering where your dreams went. Change is inevitable so make sure it's a change towards success.

1771) No matter how tough life gets, just remember that there is always a silver lining waiting for you. The only way to find it is by remaining calm and believing that success is just around the corner.

1772) Every night before you go to bed. remember that the past is behind you but still remember how far you've come. The future is bright ahead especially with the rising sun right beside your window pane.

1773) Sometimes people just need a little time by themselves so let's give them space but at the same time let's not wait around. when they're ready to be our friend then they will come back by themselves.

1774) Sometimes we get too lost in what other people think that we forget about ourselves) So let's give ourselves all the love that we need and remember that nobody can take away who you truly are inside.

1775) There isn't much in life worth getting down over when there are so many great things happening every day. And today happens to be one of those days where the good stuff is flowing pretty freely for me.

1776) At the end of each day, I close my eyes and think about all that you have achieved and how much more you owe yourself which gives me a sense of comfort knowing that you will never give up on yourself.

1777) My soul overflows with happiness and contentment and that means that nothing can bring me down because my eyes are focused on the positive side of things. And why wouldn't they be? Not me, not anybody.

1778) No one else can tell me how long I should be happy for. no one else knows exactly where I'm coming from or where I'm going. So, let's not worry about other people - instead let's worry about ourselves.

1779) Some people are going to love us while others might hate on us but the truth is, they are only projecting their own insecurities onto us. So, let's put our best foot forward and focus on what matters.

1780) We all have struggles in our lives and that's okay so the next time we fail at something, don't be afraid to get back up and try again because one day we will succeed if we never give up on ourselves.

1781) You are a child of positivity. So, no matter how much someone thinks they're better than you because they have a different religion or skin color, let's show them that you're a better person with a kind heart.

1782) I am letting go of the past. From this point forward, I'm allowing things to be easy for me. There are no challenges that I need to face, because everything is unfolding perfectly in my life right now.

1783) Let's spread happiness instead of negativity today because it creates less enemies and more friends who care for you. Positivity spreads easily so let's start with smiling at strangers on our way home.

1784) Now is not forever, change is hard but it's necessary for growth. brace those shoulders and embrace the challenge that comes our way. This won't last forever so just breathe through it until it's over.

1785) There isn't anything stopping all the greatness from happening today because today is going to be yet another fantastic addition to this story we call life.

1786) I feel grateful for all these wonderful opportunities to do things that have never been done before. Let's keep challenging ourselves!

1787) We don't have any time for negativity so let's stay positive. It doesn't matter what happens because we will always move forward from here.

1788) We all make mistakes but remember not to dwell on them because there will always be a brighter future ahead for us. No matter what happens today let's have faith that everything will work out just fine.

1789) Quit being so hard on yourself because no one can be a better version of themselves without a little push. Work towards achieving greatness and soon enough you'll find yourself living a wonderful life.

1790) Mistakes help us grow and learn from them so let's not be afraid of making them once in a while especially when it comes to being ourselves because there's no one better than us at being ourselves right?

1791) Today, and always, we feel completely safe emotionally and physically revealing our deepest desires, dreams and secrets to each other without fear of judgment because we both trust each other implicitly.

1792) We can't control what other people say and do to us but we can control how we internally feel which means the next time we get angry or upset we need to make them see that we don't want their negativity.

1793) You can't control everything that comes into your life but you can always control how you handle it so don't be afraid of taking risks because the more we fail. the more we'll learn to pick ourselves up.

1794) You should never allow yourself to think or behave in a way that makes you feel unhappy. especially when the choice is within your own control. So come on, stop sulking and show them what you're made of.

1795) When we push ourselves hard enough, our goals become possible instead of impossible. We all have the potential to be amazing individuals, we just need to stop with the negative thoughts and get it done.

1796) Let's change up our daily conversations and talk about more positive things like how beautiful the sky is or how great today feels like because there are people who can make a difference with their words.

1797) Life loves me unconditionally. From this point forward, I'm allowing things to be easy for me. There are no challenges that I need to face, because everything is unfolding perfectly in my life right now.

1798) My soul overflows with happiness and contentment and that means that nothing can bring me down because my eyes are focused on the positive side of things.

1799) The fact that success hasn't found me yet doesn't mean it won't find me at all. It just means that I have not reached it yet. I will continue pushing forward until I get there no matter how long it takes.

1800) Some of us may have experienced tough times in life but that doesn't mean I'm going to stop believing in me, just because nothing is exactly how I want it. I'm determined to succeed on some level so I will.

1801) Success isn't always easy but that doesn't mean you should give up on your dreams. If you truly believe in what you're doing then keep going until you finish. Don't let anyone try to convince you otherwise.

1802) The more we give, the more we receive which means it is important to share our love with those around us. So be sure to make them feel special every chance we get and watch how things change for us as well.

1803) We can either choose what people think about us or what our future looks like by owning everything that happens. let's be the creators of our own destiny instead of letting other people dictate how we feel.

1804) We weren't born to be perfect but we were born to become our best selves by working hard and not giving up on our dreams which means that everything will work itself out if we just do what needs to be done.

1805) Every day is an opportunity to change something in my life (whether big or small), even if all I manage to do today is rearrange the furniture. that means I'm one less day closer towards achieving my dreams.

1806) For every problem, there are always better solutions up ahead which means instead of worrying about things right now, look at the silver lining in everything by focusing on how it made you a stronger person.

1807) Just as the sun rises every morning, remember that you too can shine your light bright and stand tall throughout the day. Sunshine is only a thought away so let's find ways to stay positive during this time.

1808) Most of us are afraid to say sorry - but how can anyone forgive if they don't feel sorry first. So, let's start being more accepting of our own flaws, because it's by admitting them that we have room to grow.

1809) Failure sounds like an insult but if you think about it, failure is the best teacher you could ever have. Without failure, success would be impossible so embrace it and become stronger than you were before.

1810) I'm finally ready to take on the world and reach for my dreams because I know that nothing can hold me down. If you're worried about failing then don't be because failure is always a chance for improvement.

1811) People take advantage of our kindness sometimes but that doesn't mean we should stop helping others especially when they truly need it. we didn't choose this life so why not live it as positively as possible?

1812) Positivity breeds positivity which brings about an even greater sense of joy than before and there is nothing wrong with that, so long as I feel good right now which I do, because success is heading my way.

1813) While life may not always go as planned - "I don't have it all figured out" doesn't mean I'll fail. It simply means my plan for today is always changing so I'm open to the opportunities life presents me with.

1814) Your mistakes don't define you; they simply shape who you want to become in the future. If we never made mistakes then we'd never learn so tell yourself positive affirmations and accomplish wonderful things.

1815) Positivity breeds positivity which brings about an even greater sense of joy than before. And I'd say that's pretty fantastic. So, I will gladly continue on this path towards greatness because it so darn good.

1816) We all deserve happiness and peace in life so let's not dwell on negativity or anger because it will only bring us down. Live with love, laugh often and meditate every day. We can overcome anything if we have resilience.

1817) If you're not reaching your goals then something has to change. It's either the goal or the actions that are being taken towards it, but one of those things needs to change if success is going to be achieved.

1818) When you feel like giving up - don't, because someone else out there is fighting a battle which seems just as impossible as yours. So let' remind yourself of this by saying "I can do anything I put my mind to."

1819) The problem with some people is that they can't handle good luck. They don't know how to react to the positive things happening in their lives until something bad happens and it takes away all of their 'luck'.

1820) Change takes time but let's try our best not to let unfairness steal our smile which means even if things aren't going perfectly. as long as we give it everything we got, everything will be perfect in due time.

1821) If you want something badly enough then go for it. But remember. don't put all your eggs in one basket. Life is full of surprises so stay on your toes and hold onto what really matters because nothing else does.

1822) I'm only one person but that doesn't mean I can't make a difference. If everyone made some sort of positive impact then we could change the world overnight. So, let's all spread the love and start changing lives.

1823) It doesn't matter how tough life is because I'm going to keep overcoming adversity and thinking positively. There's too much good in my life for me to allow anyone or anything to get in the way of my happiness.

1824) Every day in life I find even more reason to smile than the last and today is no exception. It's just another fantastic addition to an already amazing story called life. And I can't wait to read what happens next.

1825) We are going to meet upsets along the way but it's ok because we don't have control over everything so just learn from other people's mistakes and keep doing our best because positive changes are bound to happen.

1826) We can learn from failure which means we should try again until we succeed no matter how many times it takes. Let's take risks because life is short and there aren't many chances if we aren't willing to take them.

1827) Life I much brighter when we dare to dream big and work towards achieving greatness in our lives because that is the only way we can push beyond our limits. You have to believe in yourself before anyone else can.

1828) Today is always better than yesterday which was always better than the day before that which was always better than the day before that. It's a chain reaction of successes, so I just have to keep pushing forward.

1829) It's okay to be different because everyone is unique in their own special way which means being ourselves is important so never change who you are just for someone else. Only change yourself when you are ready too.

1830) Life is a road and we are all travelers going in the same direction. So, let's remember that it isn't about who is getting there faster or who has been there longer because it will all pan out at the end of the day.

1831) Sometimes it's hard to accept that we need help but the truth of the matter is, no one is invincible and there are times where we can use a little extra help. So, let's ask for it. trust me, it will change your life.

1832) Lately, I've been feeling like there is a fire inside of me as it burns brighter every day. that's how much passion I have for my goals and dreams to become reality. So, let's put our hands together and create magic.

1833) We should always be grateful for what we have because there are so many others out there who are less fortunate than us. If you can't help them then at least let them inspire you to do something good with your life.

1834) Worrying about problems that haven't happened yet will only create more stress which means before we go to bed tonight let's spend some time thinking of 3 things that went well today or something that made us happy.

1835) You can try and fit in if that makes you happy but I will not be forced into changing just so they feel comfortable. This isn't about them this is about me. "You can't please everyone, so you've got to please yourself."

1836) It's okay to be sad. but just for today, then tomorrow we can do something which makes us happy and reminds us that life isn't just about what happens to you - it's also about how you choose to handle those challenges.

1837) No one else has ever had this exact version of me (and probably never will again), which makes me unique and special - especially because uniqueness is like an uncut diamond, it brighter than everything else around it.

1838) The best part about every day is seeing all the good things that are happening because there's so many of them. Why wouldn't I want to wake up every morning and know they're waiting for me? It's an easy choice to make.

1839) People aren't perfect which means they sometimes say the wrong thing so don't take what they say personally. it isn't about you at all so just stay true to yourself and let other people deal with their own insecurities.

1840) When you feel like quitting, remember what it would be like if u had quit and never tried at all. The worst thing about quitting is knowing that you gave up on your dreams when they were so close to becoming a reality.

1841) All the success in life has come my way lately. And you can trust me when I say it just keeps on coming. Not only that, but there are better things waiting for me too. So that's something else to look forward to.

1842) Doing the same thing over and over again expecting a different result is one definition of insanity but I am not insane. I can be stable in my ways because I know that inner peace cannot be achieved from changing others.

1843) Sometimes we make mistakes but what really matters is knowing how to fix them which means don't be afraid of doing something wrong every once in a while. we all need to go through those struggles for us to grow as humans.

1844) The only way you'll aim for something is if your heart says yes and not by what people say, imagine how much more amazing you would be if you did. But remember: Follow your dreams and do whatever makes your heart say yes.

1845) We all make choices which means you get to choose your reactions so don't worry about what other people do because if they want positive things for their lives, they'll get there themselves instead of depending on others.

1846) The greatest minds in history would have never achieved success if they had let their fears and doubts control them. It takes hard work to reach the top but it's all worth it when we finally start believing in ourselves.

1847) We all make mistakes, but it is how we deal with those errors that really matters. Do not fear doing something wrong from time-to-time. In order for us as humans to grow and mature, sometimes these struggles must occur. We can learn so much through trial by fire or adversity, even if just on an inner level.

1848) Being strong doesn't mean you don't have fears or doubts. it means having faith despite them. Which means don't be afraid to take small steps toward achieving your goals because every footstep starts with the right mindset.

1849) Sometimes it can be hard to remember that we're strong enough on our own because doubts will seep into us, don't listen to them though because you are strong enough. You've come this far in life for a reason, so keep going.

1850) The greatest thing about succeeding is showing people how it's done. People tend to follow what they believe they should do; therefore, if you show them that success is possible by your actions then their mind will follow.

1851) In every area of my life, the flow is effortless now it's as though everything happens by itself even when there are challenges to be met these now tend to quickly dissolve away because they no longer have any power over me.

1852) You should never allow someone who does nothing but judge, criticize and complain about their own life make you feel inferior. Because if they hate themselves, then what the hell do they have to offer you besides negativity?

1853) I don't have to be the same as anyone else- I just have to be me. And because of that I'm learning something new about myself every single day, so let's keep it moving forward. because guess what? The only way out is through.

1854) Life has been filled with so many ups and downs that it's become impossible to see whether or not I will ever reach true greatness. I don't care how long it takes, I'm going to keep pushing forward until success is achieved.

1855) Having faith simply means knowing something better will happen. (What kind of faith do I have and how do I know?) I have faith in my intuition, gut feelings and dreams because what's going on around me now is just not enough for me.

1856) People are different so let's not judge them for who they are but instead let's allow them to shine by appreciating their unique qualities because everyone has something positive about them even if it's hard at times to see it.

1857) Saying I love you doesn't have to be confined to romantic relationships or even be a friend saying it to another friend. It's also a sign of appreciation towards everything that makes us who we are. So, let's say it more often.

1858) Just because I fail doesn't mean I'm a failure as a person. We all have had our share of adversity so why not keep going forward instead of living down on yourself? We have this one life so let's make the most of every moment.

1859) All the quality qualities necessary for a healthy relationship come easily into my life now quickly creating happy blissful memories that last lifetimes together because we are both truly ready to love and create a life together.

1860) Time for a little self-talk, be gentle and kind to yourself because we all deserve better than the way we treat ourselves sometimes. You are both beautiful and wonderful so hold your head up high, don't let anyone bring you down.

1861) Don't be afraid of telling yourself that you're meant for great things because those types of thoughts never lead us astray. Everything we've ever wanted is right there waiting for us if only we had the courage to go after them.

1862) I'm not scared of failure anymore because when things get bad, all you can do is push harder. There's no time for complaining or worrying about trivial problems when there are more important things that need to be taken care of.

1863) Every day is a new opportunity to strive for more. So, if you failed yesterday then pick yourself up and give yourself another chance today. Remember that the only thing holding you back is yourself so have faith in your abilities.

1864) Life is too short to be anything other than happy, so let's not complain about our problems for another second. but instead learn from them, grow from them and move on from them. because in the end everything happens for a reason.

1865) When something bad happens, no one likes to talk about it but the fact of the matter is, we need to process if we want to move forward. So, let's make a list and bring it up. then support each other as we work through our problems.

1866) Self-doubt has been holding me back for far too long and it's time to push those thoughts aside and finally accomplish my goals. It's all about overcoming fear and believing that a better future is awaiting just around the corner.

1867) I am not going to let other people's negativity stop me from being optimistic because life is too short. We have dreams that need to be achieved so why would I waste my limited time on this planet just wishing for an easier journey?

1868) If there is money involved in a situation like a job etc. then go for it. But if not, still go for it because opportunities pop up everywhere and you should take advantage of them as much as possible so they don't slip away forever.

1869) We all make mistakes but remember not to dwell on them because there will always be a brighter future ahead for us. Just look, the sun is rising. No matter what happens today let's have faith that everything will work out just fine.

1870) There is so much good happening every day in my life now what's the point in spoiling it by dwelling on the negative side of things? Only a fool would do something like that and I'm no fool, because success is right around the corner.

1871) Let's start appreciating what we have while we have it because one day, we might not have it anymore. So, let's try to live in the moment and remember that everyone deserves happiness no matter how good or bad things might seem right now.

1872) I want to experience new things but I don't want to do that at someone else's expense because then I'm just taking away their opportunity of experiencing something that they could love. So, let's keep our eyes open for new opportunities.

1873) Today is the best time for us to start believing in ourselves, so let's make a promise to never judge people before we get to know them. Because every single person deserves the same chance at happiness even if they don't realize it yet.

1874) Every single person on this earth was put here for a reason so why do I have the feeling that I am meant for greater things? It's because my potential is limitless and no one knows what I could achieve if only they had more faith in me.

1875) Repeat this to yourself every morning, "I will succeed today because I have the power to achieve anything that I put my mind to." If you believe it, then you can achieve it. Remember, nothing is impossible as long as you don't give up.

1876) The thing about being yourself is no matter where you go, you will always have critics because people don't like change. They get used to things the way they are. Either way stay true to self or else you'll be living in chains for life.

1877) It doesn't matter if someone is rich or poor, they still need to be treated with respect and dignity which means the only person separating us is our mind because we decide how we think and feel about each other first before anything else.

1878) Sometimes we think we're not good enough but that's because we haven't seen how amazing we truly are and that's our own fault, not anyone else's. So, let's see ourselves in a positive light and use that as confidence to accomplish anything.

1879) Sometimes when life gets too much for us, we just need that little reminder that everything will be ok. We'll get through this because in times of darkness there is always light just around the corner. Stay strong and take one day at a time.

1880) When faced with an obstacle, I choose to see it as a fork in the road which means that there are two paths that I can take. the path where everything works out perfectly or the path where everything wrong. that sounds like fun so let's go.

1881) Even the most difficult of tasks will become easier once you start believing in yourself and begin moving towards your goals. The moment we stop believing in ourselves is when our lives come crashing down, so always remember to keep going.

1882) Just because I'm not waving a flag of confidence doesn't mean I don't believe in myself. It just means that I know what I can achieve if I work for it instead of expecting things to happen easily. I am worthy. I am strong. I am successful.

1883) If you focus on the negative then all you will see is negativity everywhere you look. So, let's try to not get too caught up in our own fears because every single person deserves the same chance at happiness even if they don't realize it yet.

1884) Positive thinking leads to positive results because way too many great things are happening every day for me to get down over the little stuff as a matter of fact, nothing is little anymore when the happiness just keeps on coming towards you.

1885) If you're not happy by now then something needs to change & what will that change be? It's up to me to make the necessary changes so that I can finally become happy by living exactly how I want - which is by doing things for me, not anyone else.

1886) Life isn't always easy. which means sometimes we need to take a step back and make sure we are still doing what makes us happy. So, let's try looking at things from a different perspective and believe that one day we might not have it anymore.

1887) Each minute is infinitely valuable so I use them wisely - especially when it comes to creating wealth faster than ever before. (How?) By doing one thing at a time, working my ass off & finishing what I start; because starting is the hardest part.

1888) Many people spend their lives feeling down because of the little things. But it is important to remember that nothing in this world will last forever; negativity can be overcome with positivity, and if you're always looking on the bright side then there's no reason not get what life has for offer.

1889) Accepting defeat is never an option, just learn from your mistakes and move forward with greater determination- those who fall behind only have themselves to blame for giving up too easily. Success isn't easy but it's always worth fighting for.

1890) Greatness is everywhere in my life right now waiting to be brought into the spotlight with every positive thought that comes into mind.

Well, where should I start? How about here? Right now? That sounds like a pretty good place. And guess what? It is.

1891) Don't let negative people bring down your vibes and stop you from reaching your goals in life. They won't be there for you once things get tough so don't waste time on them. Do what makes us happy and surround yourself with positivity, peace and love.

1892) It's better to ask for forgiveness than permission. because the only thing holding us back is ourselves. So, let's start using this time as an opportunity to grow and appreciate that everyone makes mistakes, because that means they're human just like us.

1893) We need to reminder ourselves why we chose our dreams in the first place even if things aren't going as planned because life is a journey with ups and downs so the only way for us not to give up is by knowing where were heading even when things get rough.

1894) There isn't much in life worth getting down over when there are so many great things happening every day. And today happens to be one of those days where the good stuff is flowing pretty freely for me Can you believe that.? Well, believe it or not, it's true.

1895) When times are tough then it's always best to remain positive about your future because nothing can hold you back from reaching greatness as long as you never give up. Remember, those who fall behind end up failing; those who pushforward end up succeeding.

1896) Let's stop putting ourselves down because we're amazing just as we are, everyone has their flaws but that doesn't mean they're awful flaws. It makes us human so embrace our differences and appreciate the fact that we're all so unique. What a wonderful thing.

1897) We can either choose to be dragged down with negativity or we can choose happiness but there is no in-between. Let's make our own choices and not let other people influence us too much. we don't need them because everything we need already exists inside of us.

1898) Those who try never fail because failure is only an opportunity for improvement. What matters most is that we rise up after our fall and always fight harder, no matter how difficult things get- you're capable of great things as long as you refuse to give up.

1899) We all have the power within us to change anything that feels negative into positive vibes. So, pick your head up off your pillow and get active, no one likes a whiny child who plays the victim. We're all capable of great things, let's go out there and do them.

1900) We are all in this together which means we need to take care of each other because that will keep us strong when times get tough. Let's be there for one another whether it is to support them or lend a helping hand because nobody should walk through life alone.

1901) Life isn't about waiting for the storm to pass. it's about learning how to dance in the rain. We can't allow something like bad weather to hold us back from achieving greatness, instead use it as a motivation to push yourself that little bit harder. You got this.

1902) I am ready for success because I know that nothing can hold me down any longer, I will work towards my dreams and reach them without giving up. We all deserve our happy ending but it won't come easily- good things take time, don't give up on yourself or your dreams.

1903) If you're looking for motivation then know that no matter how bad things get, it only means that there's still hope just waiting for you to reach out and grab it. Everything will be okay if you never give up, don't let your fears become the end of a great potential.

1904) I don't need other people to validate my opinions or decisions because if I'm not happy about something in my life then I have myself & no one else to blame. And if I am happy and excited about the direction that my life is taking then there's nothing more to be said.

1905) Everything that began has ended and everything that begins again began before - which means there's a whole lot of things going on all around me right now that I do not yet understand but let me breathe deeply & trust that everything happens at exactly the right moment.

1906) If you feel lost, alone and afraid remember there's a great big world out there full of people that care about you and want you around. Time to get back up on that horse again because life isn't always going to be easy but it's going to be worth every challenge we face.

1907) No one can tell our stories but ourselves which means writing down all of your thoughts, feelings and experiences into a journal is very therapeutic. It helps you process through emotions too. Plus, if no one knows about them then who would 'caring' take from them right?

1908) Life is a journey that doesn't always go the way we want it to because there are many obstacles in our way which means we will fall down at times but it's important to stand up and keep going no matter how hard it gets because you only live once. Let's make the most of it.

1909) I will make a name for myself one day but it all starts by believing in something greater than myself and understanding that I am capable of pushing my fears. Success isn't waiting on the other side of fear, it is already there and we just have to push through our doubts.

1910) People are always watching so it's good to make them smile & laugh & make the world a better place. (How can I do this?) By smiling more, having fun, doing nice things for people; when someone gives you attitude give gratitude instead of allowing negativity to take root within.

1911) Let's always be honest, even if things get tough - because there is nothing worse than being trapped in a lie. So, let's make a promise to never judge people before we get to know them and see that everyone deserves happiness no matter how good or bad things might seem right now.

1912) Before we can give anyone our trust, we need to learn how to trust ourselves. So, let's stop living in fear of trusting others because if you don't then you'll never be happy. Remember the only person who can make us happy is ourselves so be brave enough to do things your own way.

1913) Finding happiness in simple things like: sleeping without feeling guilty, drinking a cup of coffee while watching your favorite TV show or even lying in bed while it's raining outside. you shouldn't feel guilty about doing it. Happiness shouldn't come from someone else but yourself.

1914) I used to think that my happiness was reliant upon what someone else does or says but now I know that the only thing stopping me from being happy is my thought patterns. So instead of looking outward, I will look inward and fix my thinking because everything always starts with an idea.

1915) I used to think that my happiness was reliant upon what someone else does or says but now I know that the only thing stopping me from being happy is my thought patterns. So instead of looking outward, I will look inward and fix my thinking because everything always starts with an idea.

1916) Some people spend their entire lives chasing dreams that don't belong to them. you are the only one who can decide whether or not something has value in your life. So, let's start appreciating what we have, remembering that nothing lasts forever so make sure you cherish it while it does.

1917) If someone makes a mistake then we should always be the first ones to forgive them because we would want the same in return. So, let's make a promise to never judge people before we get to know them and appreciate that everyone makes mistakes, because that means they're human just like us.

1918) Don't waste time worrying about what others think of us, if they love us, they'll support us no matter what. So, let's not give our precious energy to someone who doesn't want it. let's save it for the people that deserve it like loved ones and friends. Those are the ones that truly care about you.

1919) Sometimes we forget how much strength we actually possess because things get tough and we start to doubt ourselves. Well, let's just take a minute to remind ourselves about all the wonderful things that we can do. Remember how far you've come and remember that you have got this. time to prove it.

1920) Sometimes in life we will be faced with challenges which seem almost impossible to overcome. but what matters most is how strong our mind is when overcoming them. So, let's try to live in the moment and appreciate that everyone makes mistakes, because that means they're human just like us.

1921) Yes life can be difficult but what matters most is how we recover from those hardships- are we going to let them stop us or are we going to push through no matter how difficult life gets? I know that I won't give up and neither should you because resting on our laurels never got anyone anywhere.

1922) Every present moment holds its own blessing, we just need to learn how to receive it. And even if we don't like what we see, remember change takes time but as long as we keep trying then someday things will get better. So, let's try waking up with an open mind, ready to learn something new every day.

1923) Life gets better with age, we just might not see it while we're trapped in our teenage years. So, let's just sit back, relax and enjoy the ride because things will start to pick up once the stressful times are over. We're all on this Earth for a purpose so let's find out what that is and get doing it.

1924) We should always be happy with what we have because there are plenty of people out there missing what they once had. If life gives us lemons, then let's learn how to turn lemons into lemonade. Remember that life is full of ups and downs so don't beat yourself up if you fall down. Just get back up again.

1925) I refuse to give up on my dreams which means right now I am going to set some goals and chase after them until I accomplish everything I set out for. Let's motivate each other to work even harder and never give up because dreams take a lot of hard work to come true and we will be remembered by our actions.

1926) We can't control everything that happens but we can choose how we react to it. Every situation has a lesson for us, if only we'll open our eyes and actually see them. So, let's learn from what happens today and make sure we don't make those same mistakes again. leaving us to grow and become a stronger person.

1927) When it comes to making changes in our lives we need to start with the little changes. Take day as it comes and enjoy the moment because you never know when tomorrow is going to be your last. Life is all about goodbyes but let's try staying just a little longer because maybe this time things will be different?

1928) We all have high days and low days. it's how we deal with them that counts. You are capable of anything you set your mind to so keep pushing at those boundaries until you can see past them. There's always another mountain to climb but only if you're willing to pull yourself up, there's no point climbing half way.

1929) Sometimes we have to just trust that the universe knows what's best for us. So why not stop worrying about understanding everything & get on board with this awesome ride? 168) Today will be great, just like every other day - so let's start making a difference & being our best selves because we owe it to ourselves.

1930) We all deserve happiness so let's find it within ourselves and spread the love, we're all deserving of it. Let's look for that silver lining because there's always one shining above our head no matter how dark things might seem. It just takes time to notice it but as soon as you do take hold of it and never let go.

1931) I am where I'm meant to be at this time in my life. (Why?) Because in order for my true dreams and desires in life to manifest into reality they must flow effortlessly through my mind and heart first. Then out of the blue they show up when I least expect them too - because when the timing is right everything happens perfectly.

1932) Always follow your heart because it will never lie to you - no matter how bad things might seem right now. there is always a chance that it could get better. So, let's try doing one more thing each day which makes us happy because life isn't just about what happens to you - it's also about how you choose to handle those challenges.

1933) I'm going to give this my all, I won't give up and if I fail then that simply means that I am walking in the right direction; you can't succeed at something without failing first. Let people call me crazy for having big dreams but they're only stopping me from achieving greatness- nothing is impossible as long as we don't give up.

1934) Don't forget to take care of yourself because if you don't who will? Make sure you get enough sleep and drink enough water to keep your spirits up. You are the only one who can make yourself feel good, so work hard during the day and play hard at night by having fun. Life is too short for anything else. So, let's enjoy it while it lasts.

1935) We all have multiple personalities depending on the person we're around or the situation we find ourselves in. So, let's celebrate our differences and not be afraid to show them by painting our own colorful masterpiece. Life is something worth celebrating, so make sure you do it because once this life is over there won't be another one.

1936) Believing in ourselves is the first step towards achieving greatness, but letting go of the past is our biggest challenge. It's not always easy facing up to what we didn't do right before but it's important to make amends if any damage was caused. So, let's leave the past where it belongs and focus on becoming better people in our future.

1937) We're all in this together, we only have one Earth and we need to take care of it. It's our home so let's not leave a mess everywhere we go. let's pick up after ourselves and recycle when the time is right. Let's be mindful of what we consume with each day and let's welcome in an eco-friendly future because it's the responsible thing to do.

1938) It's not always about the destination it's also about what happens on the journey. If you fail today, then try again tomorrow. Never give up hope and remember that no one ever said it would be easy, but they did say that it would be worth it. So, let's not give up before we've even started, instead let's take a deep breath and just go for it.

1939) We all have that friend who's always sleeping on the job. it's time to wake them up and remind them to appreciate what they've got. No one is indispensable so let's not take anything for granted because it could be gone tomorrow. So, make sure you say those three little words at least once a day because we never know when the last day will come.

1940) Worrying too much stops us from seeing the good in life, so let's just take each day as it comes and don't be afraid to enjoy the moment. Let's not beat ourselves up for being silly because that doesn't benefit anyone, instead just sit back and have a laugh at yourself. No one is perfect so learn to embrace your flaws because they make you, you.

1941) It's okay not to be perfect because perfection doesn't exist. So, let's learn to embrace our mistakes instead of denying them because they made us who we are today. We've all made mistakes, it's what makes us human. let's laugh at how silly they were instead of beating ourselves up about them. It's okay to make mistakes so long as we learn from them.

1942) "The most beautiful people I've known are those who have known trials, have known struggles and have found their way out of the depths. They're not fond of gossiping and small talk; they don't sit around judging others. They radiate a beauty that comes from inside, the kind of beauty that makes others feel good just being near them." -Elisabeth Kübler-Ross

1943) Take some time out of your day because you deserve it. You've been working hard and pushing yourself so now is the time for rest. Recharge those batteries and let go of any negative thoughts because they don't serve us at all. We need positivity in our lives because it's good for the soul. So, let's fill our cup up with love and hope and see where that takes us.

1944) It's okay if you don't know where you want your life to go. we get lost every now and then because it helps us work out which path to take. And even if we make mistakes along the way, it doesn't mean we can't fix them. Let's not be too hard on ourselves for making silly blunders but instead of forgiving them. learn from them and make a better decision next time.

1945) No matter how you feel always remember that there is a light at the end of every tunnel. There are always going to be times when we feel alone and lost. but it's never too late to start over again. So, let's try being more positive about our own potential, because life isn't just about what happens to you - it's also about how you decide to handle those challenges.

1946) I want you to know that even if your day is bad, tomorrow can be better. You have the power to change your life into whatever you wish, there are endless possibilities. And remember that if you fall down, it's okay because this is just a lesson to teach you how to walk on your own. You have the power to succeed so let's use our brains and bring out the best of us.

1947) The most important thing about you is your ability to find joy even when times are tough. Because no matter how many setbacks you might face there's always going to come a time when everything works out for the best - so let's try counting our blessings and remember that life isn't just about what happens to you. it's also about how you choose to handle those challenges.

1948) I love helping others because helping them helps me & if I can help someone save even 5 minutes out of their day then it was worth sharing what little knowledge & wisdom I have with them (List how that saves time?) By getting an idea across in 5 minutes that may have taken days to convey by someone else - they are able to move on with their day instead of wasting time being stuck.

1949) The reason why we get sad when someone says something about our appearance is because we're actually more insecure about it than we thought. It's not nice to hear something negative from someone you love and it's even worse when a random stranger does. The thing is, they don't know how much that remark has shattered our self-confidence. So, let's just give them a piece of our mind.

1950) Let's not forget to give back because it makes us feel good. When we help others, they help us in return. So, let's go out there and find someone that needs our touch of kindness. They'll learn from you and you'll feel so much better about yourself after doing something so kind. It doesn't have to be grand gestures, just the little things are what mean the most at the end of the day.

1951) Today is the first day of the rest of your life so let's not waste time waiting for things to happen. Let's go out there and do something amazing, even if someone says no it doesn't mean no forever. we just need to brush that rejection off our shoulders and keep moving forward. So, let's get out there and show everyone what we have to offer because the world needs us. We're all stars in our own right.

1952) People often wonder why bad things happen to good people. But the truth is that no one wants things to go badly for them so it's best not to think too much about such deep questions. It doesn't matter how old we get, what matters is how we grow and by taking responsibility for your own decisions - you can use this time as an opportunity to learn from your mistakes and become a stronger person because of them.

1953) Don't let anyone ever dull your sparkle, if they do just find the strength within you to climb out from that hole, and keep reaching for the stars. There's nothing wrong with floating around for a bit because it's just part of our journey, but as soon as we feel that spark again let's fly right back up there. No one is big enough to bring us down, unless we allow them to, so stay strong and remember. We're all amazing.

Financial Affirmations for every day

1954) I am financially secure.

1955) The joy I feel knows no bounds.

1956) I can handle anything that comes my way.

1957) I always have a nice chunk of money in the bank.

1958) My relationship with money is healthy and loving.

1959) I am not afraid to ask for a raise when I deserve one.

1960) Every day, in every way, I am getting better and better.

1961) I am willing to do whatever it takes to be self-sufficient.

1962) I am a genius who can handle anything that comes my way.

1963) I am easily able to save a portion of my income each month.

1964) I have more talent inside of me than I know what to do with.

1965) I deserve a good night's sleep after a long day of hard work.

1966) I feel deserving of all the abundance that life has to offer.

1967) I make a lot of money but never find myself lacking anything.

1968) I set financial goals and work hard each day to achieve them.

1969) It is easy for me to prioritize my needs and put myself first.

1970) People compliment me on my hair, clothes, and spending habits.

1971) All of my hard work finally paying off is an incredible feeling.

1972) My best is always good enough; others recognize my worthiness.

1973) being so concerned about my financial future has really paid off.

1974) Every thought I think creates a new reality for me to experience.

1975) I am willing to do whatever it takes to make my dreams come true.

1976) I measure my success by the love and happiness I have in my life.

1977) I feel confident that my financial future is secure and promising.

1978) I am financially independent and feel free in all aspects of money.

1979) My family and friends are proud of how well I handle money matters.

1980) My tax obligations are up to date and I always pay my bills on time.

1981) I am a genius, and everything I need to prosper is already within me.

1982) I value whether or not I can afford something, not how much it costs.

1983) I am able to see opportunities when they arise and capitalize on them.

1984) I have the ability to negotiate my salary and never sell myself short.

1985) My life is filled with success and happiness throughout all areas of it.

1986) The more successful I become, the less time I have for boredom or worry.

1987) I have the power, and will never give up or let anyone tell me otherwise.

1988) I'm grateful for this moment, but it doesn't define where I'll be tomorrow.

1989) As I learn more about managing money, my money skills increase even further.

1990) I can be as great as I want to be, if only I believe in my power to achieve.

1991) I deserve to be successful in all aspects of my life, especially with money.

1992) My income is higher than my expenses and I am not struggling to stay afloat.

1993) I use money to express myself in whatever way I want and make the most of it.

1994) I am aware of the impact that making good financial choices can have on my life.

1995) I am becoming more financially stable every day, as long as I keep working hard.

1996) My worth does not come from how much money I make but from who I am as a person.

1997) I am able to provide for my family and make them proud with what I have achieved.

1998) Every day, I am grateful for all of the opportunities that hard work has given me.

1999) I am able to stay grounded when thinking about money and make decisions with ease.

2000) Today I will do what others won't, so tomorrow I can accomplish what others can't.

2001) It feels good to have my own savings put away and I enjoy how it builds up each day.

2002) Money comes easily and effortlessly to me now. I am open to receive it in all forms.

2003) I am open-minded when thinking about money and willing to learn more about the topic.

2004) Spending money on others brings me a lot of joy, but it's important to save some too.

2005) I feel a sense of pride in all that I have accomplished and the time it took to do so.

2006) Money doesn't make me happy or sad, but I feel really good when spending it on others.

2007) There is no obstacle big enough to stop me from succeeding at whatever I choose to do.

2008) I am determined to build wealth so one day I can help those less fortunate than myself.

2009) I have a healthy relationship with money and make smart choices in how I spend my money.

2010) My savings account is as full as it was the day it started and every penny of it is mine.

2011) Each month, I have a budget that allows me to put at least 5% of my income toward savings.

2012) I deserve financial abundance and I trust in the universe to give me opportunities for it.

2013) Sometimes, I make peace with my past financial mistakes and work hard to never repeat them.

2014) I always learn from my mistakes because each one teaches me how not to act next time around.

2015) It feels great to invest in myself by taking a course or class on a topic that interests me.

2016) Other people are able to look up to me as a great role model when it comes to money matters.

2017) The best investment can make is in yourself by continuously learning and honing your skills.

2018) There are plenty of opportunities for everyone willing to get off their ass and go get them.

2019) I feel a sense of pride in what I have achieved when it comes to managing my money correctly.

2020) If I have problems, they are tiny and insignificant compared to the size of my heart and soul.

2021) My credit score is excellent and I have no fear of ever needing good credit for something big.

2022) When it comes down to it, the only person stopping you from achieving your dreams is yourself.

2023) It feels wonderful to succeed at saving money instead of spending everything I make each month.

2024) Today, I make a commitment to learn about how to better handle money while having fun doing it.

2025) When faced with financial decisions, I consider all available options before making a decision.

2026) I am a channel of divine energy. I use my energy to manifest the life that I desire and deserve.

2027) Sometimes, if an opportunity comes up that would cause me to overspend, I choose not to take it.

2028) As I learn more about managing my money, I look for new ways to improve upon what I already know.

2029) If I am not sure how to handle a financial situation, I ask for help from those that know better.

2030) I am proud of how much I have learned about investing my money in different things over the years.

2031) I put myself first in line when thinking about spending money and wasting it on unimportant things.

2032) It feels good to spend time away from home with people that are close to me enjoying life together.

2033) I never go into debt without having a solid plan in place that allows me to pay off my debt quickly.

2034) Saving money every month is a huge achievement and it makes me feel great to accomplish such a goal.

2035) When handling my finances, it is important to be realistic about how much I have versus what I need.

2036) I feel great about all of my savings accounts because they represent how much hard work has paid off.

2037) I value how much enjoyment I get out of spending money on meaningful things while still being frugal.

2038) I work hard at keeping my financial house in order so one day I might be able to purchase my own home.

2039) When going over my finances, I am able to keep a clear head and understand where all of my money goes.

2040) I am able to ask for help when I need it and know there are resources available to me when I need them.

2041) The most important thing in building wealth is not where you start, but rather where you plan to finish.

2042) Every little bit counts when trying to build wealth because every penny saved eventually becomes dollars.

2043) My checking account is often overflowing and there is always a healthy sum of cash in my savings account.

2044) All of my ideas are valid regardless of how others may perceive them, especially when it comes to finances.

2045) I'm grateful for what this moment brings but even more excited about all the ones still waiting ahead of me.

2046) Living below your means doesn't just benefit you financially; it also improves your overall quality of life.

2047) I am surrounded by abundance on all levels of my life: financially, spiritually, emotionally, and physically.

2048) I leave money on the table when I could be making more by taking advantage of opportunities that come my way.

2049) I live within my means and do not buy things I cannot afford or loans that I know I will struggle to pay off.

2050) I never regret trusting my instincts when it comes to money matters and know that it is always best to do so.

2051) Sometimes what you have to do isn't fun, but it has to be done because the result is worth all of the effort.

2052) When it comes to saving money, I always make sure to budget everything out and not go overboard with spending.

2053) Having good credit represents how responsible I have been overall with my finances which also means a lot to me.

2054) Although I am not perfect with money management, I know that I am always improving myself more and more each day.

2055) I am proud of my new-found financial knowledge and how much more comfortable it has made me feel about my future.

2056) I love the feeling of freedom that money provides me with. The less I worry about money, the more freedom I have.

2057) Investing in myself by learning new skills or getting certifications look great on paper when applying for a job.

2058) I realized that being broke isn't about how much you earn or spend, but rather what mindset is attached to it all.

2059) The more relaxed I am about money, the wealthier I become. I am abundant and can receive more whenever I want it.

2060) Every day brings new opportunities for me. The more I relax about money, the more money comes into my experience.

2061) I never let money stand in the way of something that is important to me and feel lucky to be able to afford it all.

2062) Just because I don't have a lot of money doesn't mean that I can't enjoy my life and appreciate everything around me.

2063) Just because my bank account isn't overflowing with cash doesn't mean I can't still celebrate all that I have in life.

2064) When faced with financial problems, I consider every option available and find the best one suited for me specifically.

2065) Combining my finances with someone else's is very stressful and makes me uncomfortable, so I keep them separate for now.

2066) I am making choices today that will positively impact my financial state tomorrow. Save now so you can spend more later.

2067) On a daily basis I am grateful for the money that I have because it allows me to live comfortably and buy things I want.

2068) Being financially secure allows me the freedom to work on achieving other life goals such as buying a house or traveling.

2069) Getting out of debt feels like climbing up a mountain; it's slow and grueling but the view at the top is worth every step.

2070) When thinking about financial problems, I take a step back and examine all of my options before making any rash decisions.

2071) Being broke sucks, but there are many like me who can relate to how difficult life is when you have no money in your pocket.

2072) I am grateful for all the money I have right now. As I focus on having more, it comes into my life easily and effortlessly.

2073) I don't need a lot of money to be happy, I just prefer having more than enough because life is easier when you have options.

2074) Reaching out for help is a sign of strength not weakness, and knowing I have a solid support system makes everything easier.

2075) Each month, I set aside a certain amount of money for savings first before spending the remainder on bills and fun purchases.

2076) I am grateful for money because it gives me the freedom to do whatever I want without worrying about how much anything costs.

2077) I am proud of how well I handle money matters because being financially responsible helps me succeed in all parts of my life.

2078) Every day miracles happen in my life, including financial miracles. I am grateful for all the money coming to me right now.

2079) My roommate/landlord/significant other understands my situation and helps me out until things get better financially on my end.

2080) Taking care of myself physically makes me feel better emotionally so I treat myself by buying something nice from time to time.

2081) When you're fit and healthy, you're able to be productive. This is essential for business, and will help me to make more money.

2082) Having a lot of free time allows me to relax and unwind without feeling guilty about wasting too much time doing nothing at all.

2083) When faced with financial problems, I take a step back and analyze my options instead of panicking and doing something I regret.

2084) My relationship with money is joyful and completely free of fear. Money comes easily to me now, and there's plenty for everyone.

2085) When faced with financial problems, I take a step back and contemplate what the best decision would be for my overall well-being.

2086) Getting over financial problems is not as stressful as before now that I know what needs to be done in order to improve upon them.

2087) My job is fun because it's a way of expressing myself and sharing what I have to offer with others. Today, as gladly as possible,

2088) I am making plans for increasing my income. I create new ideas every day that will help me gain more money, without hurting anyone.

2089) It's okay if things don't go according to plan sometimes because the only way to learn from our mistakes is through trial and error.

2090) My past mistakes taught me a lot about making better decisions moving forward without repeating the same, self-destructive behavior.

2091) Even though my bank account doesn't reflect my financial success, I know that with enough time my efforts will show tangible results.

2092) Money is a good servant but a bad master. I choose to let go of any greed, jealousy or envy so that I can experience true prosperity.

2093) When giving to others, I make sure it is something they really need instead of something I want to give them because I can afford it.

2094) In order to make more sustainable financial progress, I need focus on all aspects of budgeting from spending to saving to giving back.

2095) My personal relationships are very important and I would never jeopardize them for money at all because I value them much more than that.

2096) The money that I have now is bringing me comfort and security, and the extra advice of my accountant is helping me to plan for my future.

2097) It is amazing how much money I am able to save and spend on things by simply planning ahead. It's so easy when you know what you're doing.

2098) I am open to receiving all the money I deserve and more, as life struggles make me stronger and help me grow wiser and cleverer each day.

2099) Money is a neutral force in my life that neither brings me happiness nor sadness, but sometimes it makes me happy when spending it on others.

2100) Every day I get better at managing what belongs to me... including money. As I grow wealthy, everyone benefits from being associated with me.

2101) Happiness comes from within and not from materialistic items that cost a bunch of money that will only bring me temporary satisfaction anyway.

2102) I am consistently working towards my financial goals and targets, because I enjoy the feeling of success that comes when I receive a paycheck.

2103) Being financially free means that you don't ever have to answer to anyone or do something that you don't want to do in order to earn your keep.

2104) I am realizing that my own deeds are the only ones that can affect how much money will come to me – no one gets rich by sitting on their hands.

2105) People die with their wealth too often than not, so if I continue to save then someday, I'll be able to leave something behind for other people.

2106) People love me unconditionally- just as I love myself unconditionally. We all have our flaws, but we also have so many wonderful qualities too.

2107) Even though I can't afford it right now, I don't let that stop me from wanting to buy the things that brighten up my day and add value to my life.

2108) Figuring out how much I can save each month has been tough, but if it's challenging then it must mean that the rewards are proportionally greater?

2109) I allow abundance into my life easily and effortlessly now. It is my divine right to have an overflow of wealth, happiness, health, and prosperity.

2110) I am doing my best every day with money because it's the only way to ensure a comfortable life. Money isn't everything; but you can't buy happiness.

2111) I am growing in knowledge about money every day, and this helps me plan for the future. My savings will work hard to provide for me later on in life.

2112) It's easy to save money when you remember that everything is temporary. It all comes and goes, so why should the things that matter be any different?

2113) I am talented in many areas that I fail to recognize. I take this opportunity now to uncover my talents and use them for the greater good of humanity.

2114) I don't need a lot of money or expensive possessions to prove that I'm rich because being rich means having the freedom to do whatever makes me happy.

2115) My whole life I've been learning about money, and it's finally paying off in a big way. At this rate, my children will probably be wealthier than I am.

2116) When I learn how to make money work for me, it's amazing. It's taken a lot of effort on my part, but I can see the payoff more and more as time goes on.

2117) My new thoughts and feelings create the reality of my dreams. Every day miracles happen in my life, as long as I focus on all that is good and positive.

2118) I am doing my best every day with money, because I know that it dictates how I'll live in the future. Money isn't everything, but it sure is a lot of fun.

2119) I deserve to be happy with money in my life like everyone else. Sure, it's not the most important thing in life, but why should it be treated differently?

2120) The only thing stopping me from being rich is my ability to earn money, so I'm going to continue doing just that until one day I finally succeed big time.

2121) I deserve the best now. I accept only good things into my life now. Abundance flows naturally to me. I am wealthy because I affirm myself as being wealthy.

2122) I deserve to be happy with my money, and I'm going to go out of my way to treat myself more often. Life is too short not to enjoy things like big purchases.

2123) The most important decision you will ever make is who you allow in your life, no matter how much money they have or what their material possessions might be.

2124) When you invest your savings properly, you should see it work hard for you. This means that you can take a step back and let it do its thing while you relax.

2125) It feels amazing once you finally start earning an income because now you can do things without feeling guilty or scared about spending your hard-earned money.

2126) When I spend time thinking about my savings, it makes me so happy. It really is a lot of money, and I feel so fortunate to have been able to save all of it up.

2127) I am enjoying the fruits of my labor as I start dreaming about what's next. My hard work is working hard for me now, and even better things will be coming soon.

2128) I am working hard with money so that I can enjoy life's luxuries later on in life. If you cut back now, you'll have plenty of room to splurge when you're older.

2129) Before I go to sleep, I read an article about how to attract money while sleeping. The more I learn about the laws of the universe, the better my life will run.

2130) My money-making opportunities are increasing by the day, as well as my income. The right time to make a lucrative deal is approaching, and I am ready to seize it.

2131) The more responsibility I gain at work, the more money I can make. My boss is counting on me, which means he will give me all the opportunities I need to succeed.

2132) I am learning how to save money every day so that I can enjoy all the things I really want later on. You can't go anywhere if you don't have any money, so save up.

2133) I happily complete all tasks that come up on my path. All those who surround me are happy because we have a healthy relationship with each other and our finances.

2134) Some of the most important lessons in life are learned through mistakes, but it's our actions or reactions after making those mistakes that define who we truly are.

2135) When it comes down to it, the harder I work for money, the more money I'll be able to make because effort eventually turns into results when enough time has passed.

2136) I am taking care of my money now so that it can help me later on. It's easy to save if you just say no when tempted to buy something that isn't absolutely necessary.

2137) I am learning about the importance of money in my life, and I am getting better at managing it every day. Money isn't everything, but you need to know when to use it.

2138) It feels amazing when I buy things for myself, because it means I'm taking care of myself. If you don't treat yourself every now and again, what's the point of living?

2139) When I build my savings account slowly over time, there's something quite satisfying about watching it grow. It's nice to have a nest egg in case anything awful happens.

2140) Building wealth isn't easy, but neither is any worthwhile endeavor, and if success were as simple as working hard then everyone would actually attain their dreams easily.

2141) My finances are steadily increasing as my business expands and becomes more profitable. The more people I reach with my products and services, the more I am able to earn.

2142) The first step towards financial success is to simply stop spending money on things that don't matter and wasting money on living a lifestyle that doesn't suit your needs.

2143) I am doing my best every day with money because looking after your future is so very important. If you cut back now, you'll have plenty of room to splurge when you're older.

2144) I am grateful for all the money coming to me right now, bringing me freedom from the bondage of old beliefs. Money flows into my life with ease, abundance and prosperity.

2145) I am doing my best to be responsible with money so that I can enjoy all of life's luxuries later on in life. Sometimes you have to work for a little while before you can play.

2146) I am doing my best every day with money because financial security is so very important. You never know what life will throw at you, so having savings on hand just makes sense.

2147) I deserve to be happy with money in my life, and I'm going to make sure that happens by following a budget and cutting all of the unnecessary costs. It's easier than it sounds.

2148) I deserve to feel good about myself, and I'm going to make a point of getting what I want out of life. Money comes first – you can't enjoy yourself if you don't have any money.

2149) Living below our means affords us room in our budget to save for future purchases or invest in ourselves. We are selective with what we buy because we value our time and money.

2150) Money is nothing but a tool that allows us to make our dreams come true. Each and every dollar has spiritual value. I am rich, and money comes to me easily and effortlessly now.

2151) At this point in my life my bank account is empty, but I still have all of my internal resources available so it's just a matter of time before financial success is finally mine.

2152) When I learn more about investing, I am filled with a sense of power. By learning what works and what doesn't, I am giving myself the chance to really improve my money situation.

2153) When we start earning more, we think we can spend our way into happiness, but eventually we learn that the more money you make the more you end up spending it instead of saving it.

2154) I deserve to be happy about my savings, and I'm going to make sure that happens by using coupons and only buying the things that I need. It's a great feeling when you get it right.

2155) I'm learning so much about money every day, but I still have so much more to learn. There's always something new about numbers, even if you've been studying them for over 10 years.

2156) Once my job is decentralized, I will be able to work anywhere in the world. I am becoming more financially stable by expanding my abilities and opening myself up to new experiences.

2157) When I finally understand the financial markets and how they work, it's a huge relief. Knowing that there's someone else who can help me with money and investments would be amazing.

2158) I am doing everything I can to make sure that I'm financially responsible because it's the only way to ensure a comfortable life. Money isn't everything; but you can't buy happiness.

2159) I deserve to be happy with my financial situation because everyone else is. There's no point falling behind on your savings and investments, because it takes a long time to catch up.

2160) I know how to create a budget that works because I take control of my finances now. My income exceeds my expenditures; I allow myself to indulge in small ways because of what I save.

2161) I am doing my best every day with money because looking after your future is so very important. You never know what life will throw at you, so having savings on hand just makes sense.

2162) Getting out of debt is like climbing out from underneath a huge pile of dirt; at first it seems impossible but as soon as you make some progress, everything becomes easier and clearer.

2163) My income is increasing by taking on more responsibility, and I am finding that this makes my work days much more enjoyable. There is nothing better than knowing you're good at your job.

2164) When I make tough decisions about my finances and they work out for the best, it feels amazing. I know that it's the result of long-term planning, and that really is making a difference.

2165) I am working towards my dreams every day, and the financial gain is an ongoing perk of doing what I love. The sooner you start following your passion, the better off you'll be financially.

2166) I deserve to be happy about my spending habits, and I'm going to make sure that happens by using coupons and only buying the things that I need. It's a great feeling when you get it right.

2167) I am doing my best every day with money because looking after your future is more important than anything else. If you cut back now, you'll have plenty of room to splurge when you're older.

2168) We value our financial assets wisely. I responsibly save my money now. Spending less than you earn is the road to wealth; saving more than you spend will always be rewarded in the future.

2169) I deserve to be happy with what I have because everyone deserves a little luxury now and then. It feels great to treat yourself to something nice every now and again, I'm so glad that I can.

2170) I am doing my best every day with money because financial security is something that everyone deserves. You never know what life will throw at you, so having savings on hand just makes sense.

2171) I am taking care of my mental health every day by eating right and exercising regularly. Not only is my body healthier, but my mind is much more at ease when everything inside me is in order.

2172) Money flows through me with ease and grace. Everything works out well for me. Each time I spend money, even on simple pleasures, I get something back in return... usually something better.

2173) The literal definition of being successful is simply to have succeeded, so even though I haven't achieved everything I want to right now, I still believe that one day my efforts will pay off.

2174) I trust that as the energy of money flows into my life, it will provide all that I need. As I take responsibility for managing what already belongs to me... even better things come to me now.

2175) My hobbies and passions are expensive, but that doesn't mean that I shouldn't keep doing them even if they aren't always affordable. The cost of fun isn't equivalent to the value of happiness.

2176) The more money I have, the less important my physical needs become. As I become more prosperous, others benefit from being associated with me... because they know that they will also be rich.

2177) I deserve the best in life just like everyone else, and that includes having a proper savings account for emergencies. When life is difficult, you want to be able to depend on friends and family.

2178) I know how to set boundaries with people, places, and things. No one can make me feel loved or worthy unless I allow it. With great power comes great responsibility- so I responsibly choose love.

2179) When I think about how much money I have waiting for me from my retirement fund, it makes me so happy. It really is a lot of money, and I feel so fortunate to have been able to save all of it up.

2180) I am enjoying all that life has to offer with no fear of the future or regret about the past. Money is coming into my life in many different ways, and I will enjoy spending it when the time comes.

2181) I am proud of my efforts towards self-improvement every day, but I will continue to work hard until I am the best version of myself. This old cliché is true: you can never be too rich or too thin.

2182) When I think about how much money I have waiting for me from my retirement fund, it's so overwhelming. It really is a lot of money, and I feel so privileged to have been able to save all of it up.

2183) Charity really does feel good. Knowing that by spending time or money on someone else, I'm making a difference, lifts my spirits. There are so many people in need out there, and it feels amazing to help them.

2184) There are no problems with my finances now... only solutions. The more responsible we are with our spending habits, the easier it is to save money. I know that money comes easily and effortlessly to me now.

2185) I am doing my best every day with money because looking after your future is more important than anything else. It's nice to know that if something awful happens, I can at least rely on my savings for support.

2186) I am doing my best every day with money because looking after your future is so very important. You don't want to pass on debts and problems onto your children and grandchildren because you were irresponsible.

2187) The more time I spend focusing on my desires, the more they manifest in my life. The universe is now giving me everything that I want and desire. Life loves me, and money comes easily to those who love life.

2188) My goal is always to make more money instead of spending money on items that are not important or necessary for our happiness. My family wants for nothing because we know how to be happy without retail therapy.

2189) I deserve to be happy with my financial situation because everyone else is. There's no point in being stuck in debt when there are so many other options available to you, especially if you work hard to improve it.

2190) As I express gratitude for what money has already brought me, it exponentially increases in my life. Money flows to me from many sources. Every day more and more opportunities come my way which brings me wealth.

2191) Life has been hard for me in the past, but now it has been easy since I have learned from those circumstances. There is no need to worry about things beyond my control because they all work out in my favor eventually.

2192) We are smart about our finances; we use cash instead of credit cards. Wealth flows naturally to me now. Money comes easily and effortlessly to us now; we see money everywhere. Retirement accounts grow bigger and bigger.

2193) I am grateful for this healthy relationship with money... which further strengthens our connection. Whatever my mind conceives and believes, my body experiences. Whatever I feel in my body affects every aspect of my being.

2194) We are smart about our finances; we use cash instead of credit cards. Wealth flows naturally to me now. Money comes easily and effortlessly to us now; it's never scarce or lacking. We all deserve to be happy with what we have.

2195) I am smart about how I invest my money so that it can last forever. I take responsibility for how much money is in my bank account. We all deserve to be financially secure and comfortable with no debt and a healthy savings account.

2196) My goal in life is not to become a millionaire simply for the sake of becoming a millionaire; instead, my goal is to live comfortably with enough savings and investments built up so that I never have to worry about anything ever again.

2197) We are intelligent about our investments. The more we invest, the more money we see in our bank accounts. I avoid buying luxury items because they aren't important to me; I choose to spend my money on experiences with loved ones instead.

2198) I give myself permission to be open. I give myself permission to express my love, joy, and beauty. As I am open to new possibilities, the world opens up for me. The more I am open with my true self, the easier it is to connect with others.

2199) The universe provides for me; money flows easily into my life now. Money comes to me freely and effortlessly right when I need it. If there is a delay in manifesting money, it is because the universe knows I have better things to do with my time.

2200) Everyone on this planet is connected by an infinite source of supply. This supply never runs out; it can only multiply... like a snowball rolling down a mountain. As I focus on the abundance of this universe, it naturally transfers into my own life.

2201) I am rich, and money comes to me easily and effortlessly now. Money is not here for us to judge; it's here as a tool that allows us to make our dreams come true. I always have enough money to cover all of life's expenses- so I don't worry about the future.

2202) I trust that as the energy of money flows into my life, it will provide all that I need. As I take responsibility for managing what already belongs to me... even better things come to me now. My income keeps increasing, bringing more and more abundance with it.

2203) Before I go to sleep, I read an article about how to attract money while sleeping. The more I learn about the laws of the universe, the better my life will run. My relationship with money is joyful and completely free of fear. Money comes easily to me now, and there's plenty for everyone.

2204) My spending habits are healthy because they bring joy and nourishment to my body and mind. Money isn't earned to be saved: its purpose is to flow freely between human beings so we can all benefit from each other's talents.

2205) I will receive everything back from life tenfold. Money comes easily to me now, without my having to work for it all day long. In fact, one could say that money works for me. The more values I share with the world, the more valuable I feel. Everything I give away makes room for something better in my life.

2206) I will receive everything back from life tenfold. Money comes easily to me now, without my having to work for it all day long. In fact, one could say that money works for me. The more values I share with the world, the more valuable I feel. Everything I give away makes room for something greater to flow in.

2207) People feel comfortable around me because they know that I will never judge them or ask anything from them. Money flows toward those who do not cling to it like a child with a new toy, but those who project an attitude of gratitude toward the material things. The more we give away, the richer our lives become.

2208) It feels natural for me to help people in need because they are part of me. There is no "other" here, just existence coming through all beings continuously. you give what you want to receive, and I want to give love. As I express my gratitude, all that is mine by divine right flows back to me in generous measure.

2209) Anything I put my attention on seems to expand in front of me. The more money I make, the easier it is for me to make even more money; and this cycle repeats itself over and over again. My job is fun because it's a way of expressing myself and sharing what I have to offer with others. Today, as gladly as possible,

2210) I am smart about my finances; I use cash instead of credit card debts. Wealth flows naturally to me now. The universe rewards us for being responsible with our spending habits by always having enough money to cover all of life's expenses- so I don't worry about the future; I am safe, secure, and taken care of 100% of the time.

2211) My creativity comes up with new ideas for earning money. The more I earn, the more I can give away. All good things come to me easily now. Everything in the universe is energy, including money. If I believe it, feel it, think about it...it will be so. My life is filled with joy and laughter because of my positive attitude toward money.

2212) I am at peace with money and what it represents: freedom and power. Money allows me to travel the world, spend time with friends and family, enjoy nature, pursue hobbies, and pay bills without worrying about not having enough. We all desire for a good life- just as long as we use cash instead of credit cards so we can stay out of debt.

2213) I deserve to be well paid for my work, and I am open to receiving more tasks that fulfill me and make the world a better place. As I focus on my abundance, I allow myself to accept more opportunities like this. They come to all those who believe in their own worth and take care of their finances. The universe is abundant; there is always enough for everyone.

2214) I am a magnet for financial abundance. The more I give, the more I receive. Money comes to me easily and effortlessly now. I have enough money to save for retirement or buy whatever I desire without worrying about not being able to pay my bills. My talent is being able to live well below our means. We all deserve a luxurious life- just as long as we don't go into debt doing so.

2215) My income keeps increasing, bringing more and more abundance with it. My spending habits are healthy because they bring joy and nourishment to my body and mind.

2216) The more responsible we are with our spending, the easier it is to save money. We breathe easy knowing that our families will always come first, so we save enough money for them without worry. There are delays in the manifestation of my finances only when they are perfectly aligned for my highest good- not because there is lack or scarcity. Each and every dollar has spiritual value.

2217) We all breathe easy knowing our financial futures are never uncertain. We breathe easy knowing that our families will always come first, so we save enough money for them without worry. The more responsible we are with our spending habits, the easier it is to save money. The universe rewards us for being responsible with our spending habits by always having enough money to cover all of life's expenses.

2218) The more thankful we are for what we have, the wealthier life becomes. There is abundance in everything- not just material things. We know that experiences with family and friends are what truly matter; therefor, our incomes allow us to travel whenever possible. We all deserve a luxurious life- just as long as we don't go into debt doing so. The universe has my back when it comes to my finances. I trust myself totally.

2219) I am always financially secure, no matter what. I deserve to live a life of abundance, and money comes to me easily and effortlessly now. Money is energy; it has no power over me because everything I need always comes to me, right at the perfect time. There are delays in the manifestation of my finances only when they are perfectly aligned for my highest good- not because there is lack or scarcity. I love how abundant my life truly is.

2220) We find joy in saving money we earned because we know financial freedom will always come to us if we keep diligent with our spending habits. My family has learned the power of non-materialistic happiness, which allows us to give generously to others without worry. Money comes easily and effortlessly into my life now; it's never scarce or lacking. If there are delays, it is because the universe knows that life is short- so spend your time wisely doing what makes you happy.

2221) Our lives are abundant in happiness, love, and gratitude; the more thankful we are for what we have, the wealthier life becomes. Money is nothing but a tool that allows us to make dreams come true. We take responsibility for our own financial well-being, knowing every dollar has spiritual value. Every dollar is an opportunity to practice mindfulness in action. If there are delays, it's because the universe knows that patience is always rewarded when you invest in your future self. We all deserve to be happy with what we have.

2222) There are delays in the manifestation of my finances only when they are perfectly aligned for my highest good- not because there is lack or scarcity. Money is nothing but a tool that allows us to make dreams come true. We take responsibility for our own financial well-being, knowing every dollar has spiritual value. Every dollar is an opportunity to practice mindfulness in action. If there are delays, it's because the universe knows that patience is always rewarded when you invest in your future self. There is abundance in everything- not just material things. We deserve to live a life of luxury and opulence as long as we don't go into debt doing so. Money comes easily and effortlessly to us now; it's never scarce or lacking.

Conclusion: It's important that you remember to take care of yourself

Positive Affirmations are a good way for you to start working on your development, but the quest for personal development is infinite. It is important to take care of yourself while you are developing. By taking care of yourself, you will be able to develop yourself better.

Taking care of yourself might involve eating healthy, exercising, giving yourself time to relax or even do absolutely nothing. You need to take care of yourself in order to be able to focus properly on your journey for personal development Personal development is something that can be done at any age. There is a saying that states "you can't teach an old dog new tricks", but this is not true.

Adults as well as children can develop themselves and anyone can make Personal Development part of their lives, regardless of age. You should never feel bad or ashamed if you are still questioning things at your current age. The only way to know what you need in life is to continue seeking for your personal development.

Never give up on personal development. It is a worthwhile journey and the reward of reaching your goals is incredible!

We hope this book helps you on your journey for personal development and you are able to become the best version of yourself.

Good luck!

Feel free to contact me if you have any questions or suggestions:

bellesourcebooks@gmail.com

Join our "Relaxed Guru" email list to receive a **free mindfulness book** and stay informed about future books:

→ https://bit.ly/3bwF4vR ←

My books can't be successful without YOUR help. It would mean the world to me if you could leave a review on Amazon.

Thank you!

Imprint / Impressum

Copyright © 2021 Amelia Bellesource
All rights reserved

„Amelia Bellesource" wird vertreten durch
Tobias Schöneborn
Augustin-Wibbelt-Str. 4
46242 Bottrop
Schoneborntobias@gmail.com

Images: Licensed by Tobias Schöneborn

Copyright info
The copyrights of third parties are respected. In particular, third-party content is identified as such. Should you nevertheless become aware of a copyright infringement, please inform us accordingly. If we become aware of any infringements, we will remove such content immediately.

Liability for links
Our book contains links to external websites of third parties, on whose contents we have no influence. Therefore, we cannot assume any liability for these external contents. The respective provider or operator of the sites is always responsible for the content of the linked sites. The linked pages were checked for possible legal violations at the time of linking. Illegal contents were not recognizable at the time of linking. However, a permanent control of the contents of the linked pages is not reasonable without concrete evidence of a violation of the law. If we become aware of any infringements, we will remove such links immediately.

Manufactured by Amazon.ca
Bolton, ON